EVERYWHERE

FOR

NOTHING!

EVERYWHERE
FOR
NOTHING!

Free Travel

FOR THE

MODERN
NOMAD

 MEGGAN KAISER

meggan@bossmeggan.com

Ordering Information:
Quantity sales and special discounts are available for corporations, associations, and others. For details, contact the publisher at the address above.

Printed in the United States of America

Book Design by Ljiljana Pavkov
Cover design by Amanda Brennan

ISBN 978-1-7327965-7-7 (paperback)
ISBN 978-1-7327965-2-2 (ebook)

First Edition
www.everywherefornothing.com
www.bossmeggan.com

Table of Contents

Introduction

Why did you pick up this book? Browsing the aisles, sitting in a friend's living room, or scrolling through your search results, what made you pause and say, "Hmm … What's all *this* about?"

Let me guess: you saw the words "free" and "travel" side by side, didn't you? Did you double back to see if you were in the fiction section? Maybe you thought you were being punked.

Free travel. Could it really be true?

The short answer is yes. The long answer is the rest of this book.

This isn't wizardry, sorcery, or anything Game-of-Thrones-ery. You really are going to read about travel, and you really will learn how to make it free. At least the flying, sleeping, living, sightseeing, and eating parts.

Yep … that's pretty much all the parts.

I get it, you're already thinking it's impossible—that travel is only for the corner-office wealthy, the born-into-it fortunate, or the dusty, dreadlocked career backpacker. These stereotypes are stubborn myths that keep travel-hungry people like you anchored at home and oblivious to the "normal people" parading free-travel lifestyles right out in the open (I should know, I'm one of them).

This floating green-blue space marble we call home is huge, and our lives on it are short. Why live in a bubble, on a marble, only to be kept from seeing as much of it as possible? I mean, you can spend your money anywhere. What you *can't* do just anywhere is connect with foreigners who moments before were strangers, spend nights visiting a city's secret hot spots, or take in the sights, smells, and tastes of a place as a *local* instead of a ho-hum *tourist*.

Instead of skimming the surface with the typical "reserve, recline, repeat" vacation, why not find rejuvenation through experiences that shape and change your life? Indeed, why settle for anything less?

Don't let the "free" mislead you here. This book isn't about street busking, rickety bus rides, or hobo-ing in railroad cars. Whatever your current idea of a charming vacation is, you get to keep it. The secrets and tips you'll soon learn can be mixed and matched as you please.

Whether you're employed, unemployed, or retired; a student, a parent, or someone else, you will soon understand just how easy it is to hit the road without coming back to an empty bank account. Instead, return with the money you started with, plus a lifetime bonus of unforgettable experiences, practical skills, and travel-forged friendships.

Of course, travel doesn't always have to be about vacations. Some of you might just want to pack a bag and go away … indefinitely. That's entirely allowed. Learn here how to maintain your current lifestyle or reboot and build a shiny new one … just somewhere (read: *anywhere*) else.

Think of all the things you could do in a place you've never called home:

⇨ Run an alpaca (Yes! Alpaca!) farm.

⇨ Staff the hangover shift (a.k.a. mornings) at a busy hostel.

⇨ Declare your emancipation and become a digital nomad (your employer might actually have this as a benefit of working for them. So not only would travel be free, you'd get paid to do it!)

⇨ Bust out your green thumb and nurse someone's garden for a summer overseas.

⇨ Coach soccer (football?) at an orphanage.

But before you toss your wallet and print locations of the world's best alpaca farms, know that free travel does require some research and foresight. *Today's* budgeting will definitely affect *tomorrow's* destinations. Yes, this is a book about free travel, but no, you won't walk out the door tomorrow with the road paved in high fives and moneybags.

Start that research and foresight by reading the rest of this book, conveniently written and published for you. It's divided into five sections—(1) Budget, (2) Getting There, (3) Staying There, (4) Exploring There, and (5) Eating There—all of which are chock-full of secret techniques, ironclad guidelines, practical tips, and grandmotherly advice (What? Grandmothers know stuff!). I've also added my own revealing (all true!) experiences throughout—mainly for context and testament, but also to show that my free-travel knowledge wasn't always granted with ease or finesse.

Why take my word for it? I'm the quintessential modern nomad with a passion for unlocking this free(dom) lifestyle for others. I've traversed more than thirty countries and hundreds of cities; I've hopped aboard trains, planes, boats, buses, and automobiles; I've roomed with over twenty families in foreign lands; and I've lived abroad while having the most exciting, sleepless, fun, meaningful, and sometimes dangerous times of my life. All of my experiences have been compiled and organized into this very book to help you find the best ways to travel for free.

The world of free travel is big. But this green-blue space marble is way bigger, so don't limit yourself. Read this guide from cover to cover or skip around to the sections best for your travel dreams and goals.

And know that once you're finished reading, things will be different. Money will not slip through your fingers. Detours will appear and perhaps be taken. A week may turn into a month. A month into a year. If you expect great things and keep an open mind, your trip may even take on an improvised route of its own. This is what we modern nomads call *travel magic*—instances where people, weather, location, or timing mysteriously conspire to change your trip (maybe even your life) for the better.

Let's turn vacations on their heads: stop using them to detach, and start using them to plug in—to engage, explore, and experience all that life has to offer. To travel and experience this big ol' space marble the way it was meant to be experienced.

Saying yes to free travel doesn't mean saying no to the Real World. The two—however you define them—can coexist peacefully. In fact, the Real World is simply the world you define for yourself. Go on, do you think you're living in the same "real world" as your parents? As Kanye? As Hillary Clinton? Nope, it's aaaall subjective.

So let's just skip trying to define Real World at all. Instead, let's ask a question:

What are you after?

Your answer, should you choose to accept it, can be summed up with three words:

"Anything I want."

Because the free traveler isn't just a money-saver, the free traveler is just that:

Free.

Glossary:

For clarity and pretext, here are a few new travel concepts you'll read about (and hopefully experience) along the ride:

Travel Hacking: Strategically manufacturing and maximizing credit card rewards to cover costs ranging from airfare to hotel rooms to car rentals (without hurting your credit score).

Rental Boosting: Tapping into the global carpool network to *profit* on your car rental.

Work-Exchange: Living, working, and sharing meals with hosts (usually families) in exchange for 15 to 30 hours of work per week.

Couchstay: Staying for free on a voluntary, peer-reviewed host's spare bed or couch (as popularized by Couchsurfing.com).

Housesitting: Living elsewhere for free while taking care of someone's home and/or pets (alpacas, anyone?).

P2P (Peer-to-Peer) Sharing: Free and/or paid opportunities for peer exchanges, e.g., for accommodation (like Airbnb), local tours, bike rentals, or meals.

 ## Interlude: The Nowhere Zoo / Southern Israeli Desert

I've just stepped off a bus in the middle of the Israeli desert. It's hot. I know neither where I am nor where, exactly, I'm going.

I'm here to volunteer at a zoo, but my surroundings make me doubt its existence. A cluster of three sagging, idle buildings and a long-beached sailboat from lord knows where lie dying in the stretch of desert across the highway. Behind them, sand stretches into a haze of distant sunset-colored mountains.

If I stay on this side of the road and walk east for just a mile, I'll hit the boundary between Israel and Jordan. It rises up abruptly, a barricade of barren mountains surging up from the ground as though serving as border protection.

The bus I stepped off of moments ago blurs as it barrels northward toward Jerusalem. I head for the only buildings in sight but stop short halfway across the road. A camouflaged man dangles ten feet off the ground, tied at the wrist by a cord running between two posts. I resume breathing—it's just a mannequin—and approach.

This is the place I've come to escape mild insanity. The preceding three weeks were spent "living" within a 200-square-foot room in the southernmost city of Eilat, a place oft described by locals as the *Armpit of Israel*.

My then-boyfriend, Mr. Jams, and I have been on the road for nearly four months since permanently leaving our home in Jackson Hole, Wyoming. The first part of our trip—three months work-exchanging in France—was rough. Not just from acclimating to a new culture and lifestyle, but also in getting used to each other's constant presence.

It's in our mini-apartment that we intended to reset. It's also there that I've been passing alone the hours of 7 a.m. to 7 p.m. while Mr. Jams teaches scuba diving to tourists. I choose to stay indoors, avoiding the summer heat while pondering a question often asked and rarely answered: *What am I doing with my life?*

To avoid searching for an answer—a scary task amid all that solitude—I'd been seeking some semblance of daily productivity. I began learning yoga from an endless selection of YouTube videos; I worked on my food and travel blog; and I developed recipes in our closet-sized kitchen.

But the price of isolation was beginning to take its toll on me—and on us. Too many solo wine-drinking nights, too many lovers' quarrels, and an unexpected absence of the joy I expected to find on the road.

As I often do when in a rut, I packed my bags, kissed Mr. Jams goodbye, and made a run for it.

And now I'm on the side of a desert highway, walking by a hanging mannequin and looking for a zoo in the south of Israel. Something akin to a gas station rest stop materializes on the left. It's set back from a large awning that covers six mostly empty picnic tables and connects to a dark and empty cafeteria. I pass an exiting family with melting ice cream cones and cross the sliding doors to find myself in the Israeli equivalent of a 7-Eleven.

A blast of air-conditioning hits me as I take in the mirage of this tiny space of international snacks, cheap chocolate candies, and bright plastic soda bottles. "Matan?" I ask the cashier, a teenage girl with too much eyeliner and bottle-blackened hair. Matan is the email contact with whom I arranged this new experience—five hours of weekday zoo assistance in exchange for room and board. The cashier shrugs. I exit to linger among the picnic tables.

A young man rushes out of an outdoor corridor adjacent to the shop, and I catch him with a wave. "Matan?" He seems reluctant to stop.

"Yes? *Oh*—yes!—the volunteer," he acknowledges. "I'm a bit busy, come with me."

I follow him back through the corridor, and we emerge in a cement-floored, basin-like area. A faded wooden sign advertises an alligator habitat, but it's empty ("… died in a fire," says Matan). Scruffy men randomly posted in plastic chairs or up along doorways follow us with their gazes and cast nods when we pass.

Five mini goats join in the staring as we traverse a boardwalk situated directly above their little enclosure. The walkway passes through a row of eight one-room wooden bungalows, four on each side, facing each other on stilts ten feet off the ground.

Matan pauses, then chooses a bungalow seemingly at random. "Here!" he says, and we take the first one on the left. Walking in, my instinct is to turn and flee. Instead, I stay to watch Matan diligently scoop up two empty vodka bottles and glasses, and a discarded pair of pants. "There was a Russian here before you," is all he offers by way of explanation.

He points me in the direction of clean sheets then suggests I find Ella, the other volunteer, in the cafeteria at dinner. With that, I'm left standing alone and stupefied in my new home.

The voice, again. The question rarely answered …
What am I doing with my life?

This is a book about free travel. And yes, I want you to travel for free … but *completely* free may not actually be your thing. A piggy bank provides wiggle room. Financial reserves provide insurance. Maybe you already know how unpredictable travel can be. Maybe you don't (yet).

Either way, this section is dedicated to you. Isn't that sweet?

I know you're excited (and flattered), but before we dive into the how-tos, let's start with some context—a story, if you will, about my very first baby steps toward free travel …

Chapter 1: Harry Potter and the Berliner's Escape

My first foray into the exciting world of travel budgeting began during spring break of my college sophomore year. Instead of following the throngs of American students to party beach towns, I took off to the colonial city of Granada, Nicaragua, to study Spanish in a small school run by an enterprising pair of 20-something guys. It was a truly immersive experience, not only because my classroom was basically an entire country, but also because I arranged to live with a local family.

Studying and practicing usually involved conversations with my teacher, Juan, at the top of our favorite classroom setting—a centuries-old church bell tower overlooking the cobblestoned town square. These "school days" usually ended at a popular bar for travelers in a cheap hostel by the shores of Lake Nicaragua.

This hostel bar was where I met Hanna, a strapping, always-smiling German woman in her early 30s. She'd been traveling solo throughout Central America for the past year while teaching herself Spanish by reading Spanish Harry Potter (¡Dios mío!).

Even more impressive was her tale of escape from a rigid nine-to-five Berlin cubicle job to embark on this years-long Central American odyssey. At the time, I didn't know that time-limitless trips were things that "normal" people could do, so she promised to share her secrets if I'd sneak her up to the bell tower.

The next day, with pigeons bickering around us and our feet hanging over the bell tower's edge, I got my first lesson in becoming a nomad. It sounded pretty easy: Hanna cut costs wherever possible (*danke schön, ramen!*) and squirreled it away into what she called a travel savings account.

A year before leaving, she'd even sold her car and began biking to work every morning, including throughout the windswept, icy city streets of Berlin winter. With snow stinging her red and frosted face, she focused on her goal: freedom to travel.

But Hanna also had a strategy to reach that goal: smart budgeting. For example, she calculated that the money she saved weekly on transportation—10 euros—would cover two nights in hostels like the one where we met in Nicaragua. This was exactly the strategy I employed five years later when one of my many travel bugs hit.

Cut to: five years later.

I'd been working in gourmet food sales in Jackson Hole, Wyoming, where winter is a six- to eight-month national holiday. Feeling a gut-level need for my own travel odyssey, I set my sights on Western Europe, a mecca for the cheeses and charcuterie that had inundated so much of my professional life.

Recalling the image of rosy-cheeked Hanna riding through Berlin road slush on two wheels, I decided I could figure out another way to navigate the volatile snow and freeze of living beside the Grand Teton Rocky Mountain Range. Just like that, my beloved Subaru hit the market, and shortly thereafter, I was a local public transit expert and a few thousand dollars closer to my own escape.

Does this story have a lesson? Well, if it did, it would probably go something like this: as soon as your travel bug rears its giddy head, start saving money … aggressively. Instead of pennies, upsize to nickels and dimes. Sell what you can, forgo the gourmet, check under the couch for pocket change (if you dare), take the bus, sock it all away, and forget it's even there until you're ready to pack your bag.

Don't even think about a target number for now—it's a wildly flexible thing that may change over time. Just save. The numbers will reveal themselves as your planning and travel take shape.

Dankeschön, Hanna!

Chapter 2:
The Here and Now of Budgeting

Show of hands: how many of you believe that effective money management means not getting that extra flavor shot in your fancy coffee every morning? I know. It sounds responsible and disciplined. And while it may save you a few bucks here and there, it won't get you much farther than the suburbs.

That's okay, because let's face it, budgeting wasn't necessarily something we learned as kids. If your parents, friends, or the strangely enlightened homeless man on the corner taught you about money (lord knows the schools probably didn't), kudos to them. Failing that, it's up to you and you alone to learn savvy spending habits.

That was the bad news.

The good news is you can start this process as soon as right now. So grab a pad of paper, a pencil or pen, or whatever note-taking app you use and let's DO this thing.

There are three initial steps to smart spending. The first two involve mindset more than nuts and bolts—effective money management takes discipline, commitment, and knowing yourself very, very well. The last step is about seeing the big picture so that you'll know what to do once the money adds up.

Step Two: Define Your Values

"Hey Meggan! Aren't you forgetting a step?"

Very perceptive, dear reader. But we've already covered Step One. Courtesy of smiling Hanna, you learned to just. start. saving. Find the opportunities and seize them. You'll figure out what to do with those extra dollars later on.

Congratulations. Step One is done. You're saving for travel!

This next step is a bit more, shall we say, cerebral. Take a moment to reflect inward. Think about your primary values—the stuff that gets you out of bed every morning—and write them down. Go on, make a list: What's supremely valuable in your life? On your deathbed, what do you want to say you lived for?

Maybe your list includes stuff like:

⇨ career advancement   ⇨ marriage

⇨ skills development   ⇨ family

⇨ travel   ⇨ improving health and
                              well-being
⇨ volunteering

Now put those values in order of importance to you. How do you want to live your life? If you're reading this book, we can assume that travel is pretty high up there. And surprise, surprise, that's the value we're going to focus on.

So here's a cup of logic for you to drink: if travel is one of your highest personal values (it's right there on your list!), but you're not doing it as much as you'd like (if at all), then it's safe to conclude that ... you're not living in accordance with your highest values.

BAM!

Mind blown.

So ... what's up with that? How is it you've placed so much of your *own* value on travel, but there you are, not doing it? Why the disconnect between value and action?

Consider this: you've been stuck in a common pattern put in place from early life (parents, school, TV, etc.), and it feels vaguely like you're not in the driver's seat (college, career, PlayStation, marriage, family, mortgage, PlayStation, career). Is that you?

Or maybe you've come to believe you don't deserve life-changing experiences like world travel. Or worse, that you *do* deserve to be unfulfilled.

Or could it be that you just don't realize any of this is happening simply because it's become so ingrained and habitual that it's practically on autopilot?

Whew! What does any of this have to do with freakin' budgeting?

Well, it's all about awareness of your real-life actions and how adjusting those actions can help you live your values and get out to see the world. Prioritizing your values helps you expose behaviors and habits that don't serve them.

(Make that list, I mean it.)

True story: according to the US government, I've lived at the poverty line for the past decade, yet I've never felt like I'm struggling for money (okay, maybe once or twice). I've covered many miles in that time without a sense of financial lacking, because I'm careful to spend my time and money in accordance with my values.

So, I'm sorry, the whole *I-don't-make-enough-money-but-actually-probably-I-do-make-enough-money-but-I-just-really-don't-actually-know-what's-going-on-here* excuse just doesn't work for me.

Look hard at your free time and ask yourself if there's more you could be doing to create *lasting* fulfilment, not just temporary enjoyment. Maybe you don't need the newest version of Grand Theft Auto. Janet will be fine if you skip post-work chardonnays for a month. The guys will manage if you forego a wing night or three, right?

Happy hour and gaming aren't in the top-five list of your values. Take Janet for a walk instead. Crack open a cold one with the boys at your place—and make it BYOB. This is basic habit recognition and action. And this is Step Two in getting outta Dodge with a nice bit of cash to your name.

 INSIDER INFORMATION: You're creating extra time *and* extra money—want to know how to make that dough grow? Take that time and educate yo'self! Read **Money: Master the Game** or **Rich Dad, Poor Dad**—two of my faves for money mindset and action.

Step Three: Pay Attention

If you've never tracked your expenses before—in a spreadsheet, web service, or mobile app—you should. It's eye opening. Try it. Track your spending with apps like Expensify, Mint, or PocketGuard for a month or a year and see where your money goes.

Once you have a detailed overview of your personal spending habits, it's easy to figure out where to make cuts to get you closer to a walkabout. Is it time to skip the vanilla lattes? Can you go without unlimited cell phone data? Do you really need to drive seven days a week?

Think of every purchase you make today as a missed opportunity in the future. Your neighborhood economist might call this "opportunity cost." The $25 monthly manicure *now* means no más to Barcelona's La Sagrada Familia *later*. Trivia night with friends? You could be slaying cider on a pub crawl in Ireland! Premium cable subscription? Don't you want to taste authentic Balinese nasi goreng!?

I think you get the point.

Tangible Tips for Makin' Bacon

The easiest way to save money is to have a job. Or two. Or a trust fund. Duh. But I'm not here to tell you to add something to your life equation to increase your savings. I'm here to tell you to start taking away. You don't have to revamp your world, just stop spending so much! Tell yourself and believe that you do not have money to spare, and you will stop spending like you do.

Bonuses, extra tips, or a salary raise should not be seen as "extra" money. Extra money is never "extra" money—it's future money. Face-melting, globe-trotting, amazing-adventure future money.

Just put your head down and think about what you truly want. For starters, decide if you're more of a cash or credit spender. For me, the less I see and handle my money, the less I think I have. I spend accordingly. For others, it's more useful to handle cash instead of credit or debit cards. Be honest—which are you?

 RETHINK IT: If you avoid credit cards due to issues with gratuitous spending, I *strongly* suggest finding a financial coach or doing serious self-coaching to get a handle on things. Why? Because credit card purchases *earn* you money. As long as you're buying things that you truly need, these earnings are like *free money*. More on this in Part Two.

Overdo Cash Spending? Do This:

⇨ All cash-in-hand goes straight into a piggy bank.

⇨ This piggy bank is emptied with weekly scheduled trips to the big-boy/girl bank.

⇨ In the meantime, retain a well-calculated allowance from your stash for necessary spending.

⇨ Budget cash into categorized envelopes—"groceries," "rent," "fun," etc. Then, when it's gone, it's *gone*, baby.

⇨ If you find yourself dipping into your envelopes too often, use a lock and key to dissuade yourself (sounds crazy, but it works).

⇨ Utilize a direct deposit system with employers.

Credit Racker? Do This:

⇨ Ask a trusted friend to hold onto your cards and only let you spend on needed items (but don't you go memorizing that card information!).

⇨ Or, keep your cards at home and only carry with you the cash you plan to spend.

⇨ Don't store your credit info online (this'll make impulse buys more difficult).

⇨ Use browser extensions and apps to block online shopping sites.

⇨ Otherwise, cancel your credit cards and spend only with cash.

Hacking Your Bank: Legally and Other Totally Legal Moves

Set up a monthly transfer from your "disposable" money account (usually a checking account) into a specific travel savings account and don't touch it! Even if you can only safely spare $50 per month, that's $600 in one year for travel.

Ensure that your savings accounts have competitive interest rates. Credit unions often offer rates 500% higher than the national norm. 500%!

Consider ending subscription services for entertainment expenses, like kitchen-sink cell phone plans, premium TV, and monthly music streaming. Do you really need two-day shipping? Can you use your local library's free video streaming service or ebook borrowing?

While abroad, there are prepaid SIM cards that will probably work with your device—research them and consider cancelling your local phone plan if you'll be away long term. Apps like WhatsApp and Skype make long-distance communicating easier than ever.

 TECH TIP: Consider setting up a VoIP (Voice Over Internet Protocol) phone number so if people call or text you, you'll receive it through your Internet-connected phone or computer. The VoIP industry is competitive and it changes every year, so search online for "Best VoIP" to get the latest info.

There are also tons of ways to get international WiFi for your phone at a relatively low cost. You can use apps to find WiFi near you (check **WifiMap.io**, **Fon.com**, or **Instabridge.com**) or take WiFi with you by subscribing to a Virtual Private Network with a service like **TunnelBear.com**.

Chapter 3:
Crystal Ball Budgeting

You've laid the groundwork, now let's consider the brass tacks of your travel future. Travel budgets vary depending on the type of trip you hope to take. And let's be real: travel tends to bring unpredictable expenses no matter how long you're away.

The solution? Create a Crystal Ball Budget: list *any* and *all* potential expenses. Add them up. There you go. *Maaaagic!*

No item is too small for your Crystal Ball Budget, and no headscarf is too snazzy to wear while doing it. Don't hold back. In fact, do this with a worst-case scenario mindset; understanding the full cost of everything ensures preparation at worst, and extra money at best.

If too many numbers make you dizzy, then sure, take what you have upon launch and see how far it gets you. But the less you pay attention to *micro*-financials, the more easily they accumulate and turn into *macro*-financial problems.

Up-front costs are just as important to consider as what you might encounter once on the road, and luckily they're easier to anticipate. As you read through this book, you'll find out how to avoid many of these costs, but it's still a good idea to know what you might spend in case plans fall through. Better safe than sorry.

The following **anticipatory travel costs** might show up in your free-trip planning:

> **PRO TIP:** Consider adding $150 padding to your budget for every time you enter or exit a country. This is an emergency fund for unforeseen troubles with transport or immigration. It's not a small number, but it's realistic. Ideally, you'll never have to use it!
>
> Fact is, when you're operating from free, it's smart to have some fallback "sh*t happens" cash—just in case, well, sh*t happens. This cash will also provide flexibility when, for example, you've got your sights set on a month or more in Europe after spending a year in Southeast Asia.

⇨ Registration prices for work-exchange, housesitting, and other travel-friendly programs.

  ⬤ Workaway and HelpX each charge about $30 for two years.

  ⬤ Housesitting website membership fees (free to $100ish).

  ⬤ Couchstay registration fees, if any.

⇨ Transportation

- Base costs of arriving in and leaving a country.
- Entrance and exit taxes (it's a thing in some countries).
- Transport expenses within a country.
- Car rental
  - Consider gasoline or petrol costs and tolls (which are often more hefty than you'd expect!). A websearch for "toll road calculator" and "fuel calculator" for your desired country will generally enable you to predict a number for these expenses.
- Rideshare or carpooling availability
  - Often, you can only guess whether your desired route will have available drivers or riders, but placing yourself along a popular route will boost the odds.

⇨ Visa expenses (if applicable)

- Visit your home country's passport issuing office or its travel website for relevant overseas costs.

⇨ Health Care

- If your health care doesn't cover your travels, consider canceling it (for long trips) and signing up for traveler's insurance, which is often lower-cost.
- Many countries offer excellent free, tourist-inclusive health care.

⇨ Other Insurance

- If you're paying for unnecessary insurance while traveling (like auto or renters), try to cancel or put it on hold.

⇨ Food

- Playing tourist? You'll be paying for most of your food—minimize costs by reading Part Five.
- Housesitting or work-exchanging? You may be paying for groceries, or it may be baked into your "room and board" arrangement—more on that in Part Three.
- Websearch "daily [gluten-free, vegetarian, vegan?] food budget in [country name]" to find articles or bloggers that reflect your eating style or needs.

⇨ Tourism

- My advice is to check out the cultural "big guns" of a country while you're there, even if some do cost money. Everyone should see the Eiffel Tower or The Great Wall of China at least once.

⇨ Gear

- Some work-exchanges ask that you bring specific gear like a tent, gloves, or rubber boots (but some will have loaners if you forgot to pack them).
- Hitchhiking or camping gear.
- General travel sundries like weather-related gear, lotions and potions, etc.

⇨ Little "Thank You" Gifts

- When staying with a host, bring something that says "thank you for welcoming me into your house." A bar of chocolate or souvenir from home should do the trick.

No matter how generous your travel budget, a free trip is still possible. A cash surplus on either end of your travels is just a bonus. Put it in your travel savings account for the next excursion. (Hey! Good thinking!)

However you look at it, cutting back on random spending in order to save, invest, or spend wisely means that you'll have more money to spend on things you truly value. That's what we call maximizing that dollar dollar bill (y'all).

After getting the "B" word on-lock, what's next? How do you actually plan it all? Figuring it out from here can be overwhelming because, honestly, possibilities are endless! So, how do you narrow things down?

The first thing we look at is timeframe. What do we do with a time-frame? *We fit things into it!* When do we do it? *Now!*

Maybe you already have a travel timeframe in mind, or maybe you're reading now to figure that out. Those are both great starting points! Whichever it is, the following chapters on Getting There will teach you what to expect from your finances therein. We're not just talking about the trip you're about to take, we're also deep-diving into future journeys so you can create multiple trips of a lifetime no matter the circumstances!

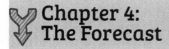

Chapter 4:
The Forecast

We've all dreamed about the perfect trip ...

Everything has fallen into place. The unexpected is nonexistent. All your foreign ducks have aligned like stars in the night sky ... And then you wake up in a semi-cold sweat, muttering something about stars and ducks, and you realize that there is so. much. planning to do!

If you're taking a trip to unfamiliar countries, your best waking strategy—especially if you prefer keeping your money belt zipped shut—is to do your research and plan accordingly. Sometimes weather, culture, and infinite other factors simply don't cooperate with dreams. Weigh the following **logistical factors** prior to finalizing plans:

⇨ Destination
⇨ Timing
⇨ Price of foreign visas
⇨ Culture and politics
⇨ Financial requirements

It's a short list, but there's a lot going on when you drill down on each one. Don't be overwhelmed—there's no test. Our goal is to understand each item individually and how, collectively, they'll become your one solid travel plan.

Let's get started!

Destination

Whatever the length of your trip, weigh destination options early. While traveling short-term makes it easier to pre-plan daily itineraries more accurately, long-term travel generally calls for plans to be made anywhere from a year in advance to hours before departing. Yes, that's a large variance, but it's really up to your individual resources and desired pace. Either way, having a well-researched understanding of logistics for each destination helps you decide what's best.

If you already have a travel timeframe in mind, remember: try to keep it flexible. By the end of your travels, you may end up with more money than you originally budgeted for, more new friends around the world, and an insatiable desire for more travel.

Work It: The Route Backbone

If you don't already know where you're headed, write a list of ideal locations and prioritize by what and where you *can't* miss for your next trip. Are you dreaming of a Central American adventure? Maybe a North African experience? Maybe you want to focus on one specific region, maybe you want to bounce around like a jet-setter.

 INSIDER INFO: The most renowned city isn't always the best to visit. For example, most travelers want to visit bustling Paris, but what about Leon? It's less-expensive, rich with culture, and the culinary capital of France! Web-search "best cities off the beaten track in [country name]" to find your secret dream destination.

If it's more than a couple regions or tourist attractions, create a vague route backbone by marking your destinations with a pen, pin, or marker (or crayon! Colored pencil!) to visualize the big picture. Structure your route backbone with an eye toward geography. Try to avoid doubling back on a route you've already travelled (and possibly already paid for) and remember that transport costs will generally be cheaper if you can maneuver closer to your next destination while traveling.

RETHINK IT: If you can't go abroad, no worries! You'll soon learn of the likely free-travel options waiting in your backyard. Apart from expanding that public spirit, staying national can also save you a nice chunk of cash.

If free accommodation is a prerequisite for your route, you'd better have both plans A and B in your route backbone. Forecast host options along the desired route (we'll cover host-scouting in Part Three), because it may turn out that there aren't enough free options where you want to go. It ain't a free trip if you're forced to take refuge in a hotel.

The route backbone is an outline to anchor your travel plans while allowing for some flexibility along the way. Why flexibility? Forrest Gump and I have already said it: sh*t happens. And when it does, staying flexible in your planning often saves the day. It's also okay to invoke those powers of flexibility to intentionally plan while on the road; this is how travel adventures begin!

Here are some relatively random but totally awesome country-to-country route backbones to consider:

```
            Spain - France - Italy
       Austria - Czech Republic - Poland
         Montenegro - Serbia - Bulgaria
      Romania - Lithuania - Latvia - Estonia
Trans-Siberian Railway through Russia (fewer options overall,
                but what a trip!)
           Norway - Sweden - Finland
          Mexico - Belize - Guatemala
         Bolivia - Argentina - Paraguay
       Indonesia - Borneo - Philippines
         Cambodia - Vietnam -Thailand
          Sri Lanka - India - Nepal
         China - South Korea - Japan
          Israel - Turkey - Greece
        Nigeria - Mauritania - Morocco
         Zambia - Kenya - Tanzania
              US East/West Coast
```

Timing

From weather, to host availability, to pricing, to departure, timing plays a huge role in travel considerations. And in my experience, nothing affects travel timing more than climate. Do your research on typical weather conditions along your backbone route and the surrounding areas.

TALES FROM THE ROAD: I planned a July farming work-exchange in France's northwest coast, which is beautiful and sunny in the summer, right? Nope! Sunny beach weather it was not. Instead of swimsuits, sunscreen, and surf, it was scarves, sweaters, and showers. In July! *Mon dieu!* (*yeah, yeah,* first world problems.)

How does timing relate to free accommodation? During cold or wet seasons, work-exchange hosts have fewer job options for volunteers, but also fewer applicants to those jobs, so your chances for free room and a gig get better.

Housesits, on the other hand, practically multiply when homeowners seek to escape to warmer climes. The number of couchstays also increases during poorer weather when there are fewer tourists, so this increases your odds of finding a good place to hunker down.

Weather is less of an issue if you intend to stay indoors most of the time. A rainy, writing-filled November spent housesitting a cozy stone villa in Tuscany doesn't sound so bad. But a work-exchange herding sheep in the hills of a wet and chilly Turkish winter certainly *does*.

 TALES FROM THE ROAD: When played right, visiting certain areas during the off-season is a brilliant strategy—even as a regular ol' paying tourist. Here's the scoop: many locals decisively stop vacationing when the calendar marks the end of summer. Thing is, actual summer weather doesn't always abide by these dates (what a rebel!).

It's like that one unseasonably warm and sunny autumn when I visited the pristine island of Monemvasia, Greece. Officially, tourist season had ended, so the typically visitor-besieged town was empty. Luckily, I know a thing or two about how to read a basic weather forecast. Seeing that the beautiful weather was meant to last, I arranged my stay and had the tourist-free town to myself (at off-season pricing)!

Visa Considerations

Do you know what a Schengen visa is? For me, it's that one essential tidbit of information I didn't have at the outset of a European free-travel work-exchange trip. The majority of European Union member countries are within something called the Schengen Area, an area in which most foreigners cannot stay for more than three months. It's the visa equivalent of a countdown timer … and my time in the Schengen Area had come to an unexpected close.

Turned out I would have to spend three months outside of the area to be let back in. *Here's* where a flexible backbone route would have come in handy. Because I anticipated *all* my travel taking place in the Schengen Area, my leisurely idealized route through Europe suddenly became a fitful zigzag.

To minimize travel costs, I escaped to relatively "local" non-Schengen countries like Israel, Turkey, and the UK. Since I wanted to stay at least three months in each country, and I didn't like to plan more than three to six months in advance, all I really had to do was arrange one country at a time. In a way, this made the overall planning feel less overwhelming. But boy did I learn my lesson about travel pre-planning and re-pre-planning!

If you don't want to fall into the same trap, check visa requirements for all locations you plan to visit *before* you visit them! Check online first and foremost. Your country's passport issuing office or the destination country's tourism authority will outline relevant visa information.

When in doubt, call that country's embassy—sometimes online information is outdated. Case in point? With my three months in France running out, I purchased a ticket to Cyprus, since its government website claimed it was not a Schengen Area country. Unconvinced and once-bitten, I called their embassy to confirm their Schengen status. I was informed that although they were not a Schengen Area country, they

ACHTUNG! Some immigration agents might want assurances that you're not some vagrant intending to live and work there illegally. They might ask for "proof of support" or "means of subsistence." This is to show that you have enough money to support your travels.

Bring relevant documents, such as proof of employment (pay stubs), a personal bank statement showing finances for at least the last three months, or proof of prepaid accommodation. You might also be asked for proof of exit (your departure ticket). If you don't have one, you can buy a refundable ticket to show officials upon arrival. And then you can cancel it once you've been let through immigration. Boom! (Just make sure it is, indeed, refundable.)

did follow Schengen visa rules. Luckily, I was able to cancel my ticket for a refund. Even governments procrastinate. (Surprised?)

Culture and Politics

Planning to travel to a country without knowing a thing about their culture, language, or political climate? Please don't do that. Don't go into a country blind.

First and foremost: is the destination safe? Some of them are a "no-go" on basically every list out there, unless it's a list called *Best Places to Risk Emotional Strife and Physical Danger*. But if you're pining to go somewhere and unsure of their safety status, just websearch "travel advisory for [county name]." Your own government should have this information readily available. Safety is paramount, *especially* for the adventurous spirit!

The next thing you should know is the destination's culture and language. Don't be that traveler who uses the wrong finger gesture in a conversation. You may get some laughs … or you may just get an angry rant you can't understand or apologize for. Or maybe you'll just look really silly to a lot of people.

Lack of research *also* boosts the odds of getting a chilly reception from the locals, which in turn creates a barrier to a positive travel experience for *you*. Go on, be selfish—learn things!

Quiz time: Culture Club

1. In what countries should a female tourist wear a headscarf?

    a. Iran

    b. Saudi Arabia

    c. Turkey, Iran

2. The amount of suggested eye contact when meeting someone new in western countries is considered what in China, Japan, or Vietnam?

    a. Also normal

    b. Disrespectful

    c. Flirtatious

3. What does an outward-facing "peace" sign mean in England?

   a. "Peace!"

   b. "Later!"

   c. "Screw you!"

4. What does a thumbs-up mean in the Middle East?

   a. "One minute"

   b. "Up yours!"

   c. "Great job!"

Answers: 1. (a), 2. (b), 3. (c), 4. (b)

Learn these things. If you're not willing to adapt, then stay home and volunteer at your cousin's elementary school.

Useful online search terms to explain **cultural greetings and customs** are:

   ⇨ Traditions/etiquette/obscene gestures in [country name]

   ⇨ Things to know about [country name]

Don't forget the communication component. How difficult is the language in the places you're considering? Can you get by without learning it or will you have to acquire at least *some* traveler phrases? Are you *willing* to learn? This should impact your decision!

 TALES FROM THE ROAD: The French tradition of *"faire la bise"* (cheek kissing) is forever my personal challenge. Is it two cheek kisses? More? Who starts? What if there's an accidental lip lock? Was that even an accident?!

I always manage to fumble this exchange. I can never figure out if a newly introduced person will go in for the kiss, or—since they know I'm American—try to shake my hand instead. Usually, once I realize they *aren't* going for the kiss, it's too late—I've already leaned in and puckered up. At that point, I just hover awkwardly while pretending to inspect something on the far wall.

Cultural rule of thumb: Let the country native decide, and follow suit!

Financial Requirements

Unless you're planning to pay for accommodation, transportation tends to incur the heaviest costs. The cheapest option is to hitchhike, or you may prefer something more predictable (and safer, in some areas), like a bus or train.

To best anticipate transportation expenses along your backbone route, look at the size of the countries or regions in which you're interested, along with their distances from one another. Do your preliminary scouting to know which methods fit your budget—some countries are cheaper to get around, or to get to or from. Search "getting around in [place]" and "getting to [place] from [place]" online to get started.

There are plenty of other financial considerations depending on where you're going and for how long: visa costs, travelers insurance, SIM cards, and much more. If this is a major concern of yours, I recommend re-reading Chapter One (The Here and Now of Budgeting) a couple of times, or until you're comfortable with how you plan to manage expenses throughout your travels.

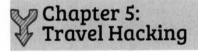

Chapter 5: Travel Hacking

A word of caution: The following chapter involves the use of (usually) more than one credit card and precise financial budgeting acumen. If you lack a disciplined approach to finances and budgeting, please do not use these methods. Instead, I urge you first to develop more rigorous budgeting habits and greater control over personal spending.

Now that you know where you're headed, let's talk about getting airborne. Covering long distances by plane may be costly, but it's also fast. Though some airfare deals are found as easily as scrolling through your inbox, becoming truly skilled at tracking them down can be as daunting as learning a new language.

In fact, it *is* like learning a new language. But it's not as hard as you think. Absorb the following information and you will absolutely save hundreds, if not thousands, of dollars on airfare.

There are two main ways to save on airfare. One is simply through general research, planning, and smart purchasing. But the other, known as "travel hacking," is the *coup de gras*, the big gun, and the reason you read the word of caution at the top of this chapter. I'm bringing it out first because, if done properly, it is *very* effective.

Few people seem to know about travel hacking. The ones who *do* are often regarded as magicians. Indeed, it may be free travel's most lucrative secret. The gist is to strategically manage credit card spending so that points, miles, and signing bonuses create and accumulate value far surpassing everyday expenditures. These rewards are earned from spending just like you normally would, and they can also fully fund your travel—anything from airfare to lodging to car rentals.

Is it *legal*? Is it *safe*? These questions aren't so unreasonable. How can opening streams of credit cards to maximize rewards be fiscally responsible? But the fact remains: thousands of credit scores have actually *risen* during the process of travel hacking.

That also being said … as alluded to in the caution above, do the work to get your budgeting and spending under control. You need those credit card rewards. Self-control is a muscle—it can be exercised and strengthened. Just like there are driving teachers, there are plenty of teachers out there in book, blog, and human/professional form to help you with money mastery. There's no good excuse to close the door on this free money!

Off the soapbox, on to how credit card rewards work. Let's take an example from my life: I earn two miles for every dollar spent with my current card, and each mile is worth one penny. That means spending $15,000 per year translates to 30,000 miles. That's $300 dollars in pennies (er, miles) for the first year, and $205 per year after that once the annual fee of $95 kicks in.

But where travel hacking *really* pays off is with signing bonuses. In my case, if I spend $3,000 in the first three months, the credit card company awards me an added 40,000 miles. Remember—each mile equals a penny, so that's a $400 bonus to be used either as statement credit (to pay off my balance) or toward future travel bookings! Since I timed the card application with a few big impending expenditures, I earned $400 by spending on things *I already needed to buy*.

In the world of travel hacking, the terms *points*, *rewards*, and *miles* are often used interchangeably. So, what's the difference between them?

Instead of defining them, just think of them as "cash" awarded to you for using that card. The difference is in their *translated value*, which is what $1 of spending *translates* to in points, rewards, or miles value. This amount differs according to various cards' terms, so make sure you inspect said terms from top to bottom.

While I staunchly won't advise you to spend unnecessary credit card money just to get more rewards, I'll soon show you how to "manufacture" purchases in order to meet a card's signing bonus. Otherwise, travel hacking is only best if you *naturally* spend the amount that will translate into a profit in points or miles.

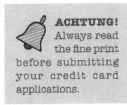

ACHTUNG! Always read the fine print before submitting your credit card applications.

This profit is called a *break-even point*, which is calculated by subtracting the card's annual fee from the annual value of the points or miles received. If the value of the points or miles received is greater than the fee, then you're profiting. Remember: since you pay off your cards each month, you're not racking up monthly interest; so, the annual fee is the only additional cost of the card.

That may sound uber mathematical, but you'll see how easy it is once you begin looking at the terms of individual cards. The trick is finding a credit card that works for your spending habits. Some cards particularly reward lots of grocery store purchases, some airfare, some fuel, some specific websites, and some restaurants. Everybody spends differently, so ironing out the details of your spender profile and appropriate credit card is best undertaken with a personalized internet search session. Good luck!

Travel Hacking Recap: Do you meet the following requirements?

1. You aren't in debt.
2. You pay your bills in full each month.
3. You can hit the spending break-even point.
4. You can capitalize on those signing bonuses (without creating unnecessary purchases).

A Guru Speaks: Jason Moore, Founder, ZerotoTravel.com and LocationIndie.com

If travel hacking still seems scary, I've brought aboard a travel hacking wizard to ease your worries. Jason Moore, founder and head honcho at **ZerotoTravel.com** and **LocationIndie.com**, is renowned in the budget travel world and aptly refers to his lifestyle as *Wanderliving*. I discovered Jason through the *Zero to Travel* podcast and quickly became addicted to his ever-cheery attitude and down-to-earth personality. The proof is in the pudding, so listen to his podcasts at **Zero To Travel**, **Trekking Nepal**, and **Location Indie** along with following him online.

Is he a kindred spirit to vagabonds? He may well be the king. Truth is, with over 20 years of experience, his travel hacking know-how is hard to beat. Here's the lowdown, according to Jason!

Everywhere for Nothing (EfN): First things first: How would you describe travel hacking to the complete newbie?

Travel hacking involves working within the existing rules set up by airlines, credit cards, and hotels and using them to your advantage to earn free travel including flights, lodging, and other upgrades.

EfN: What are some key points to convince wannabe vagabonds that travel hacking is worthwhile?

As far as using credit cards to earn free flights, it's only worth getting into it if a) you have zero credit card debt and b) you are fiscally responsible. Otherwise, the "free" flight could cost you thousands more in fees.

BUT ...

If you are carrying a credit card around and using it responsibly and NOT earning travel rewards, points, or miles, then you are pissing away free travel opportunities.

At the very least, if you are already flying and sleeping in hotels, be sure you are signing up for their free rewards programs and getting credit for those flights or hotel stays. You might be surprised at how quickly you can earn free hotel nights or flights.

EfN: I just don't spend much money. Do you have any recommendations that would enable me to meet reward bonus minimums?

There is something called "Manufactured Spending," which is just a fancy term for spending money without spending it. Let's call it what it is ... legal money laundering!

Strategies are ever-changing. The best place to stay up-to-date is the sub-forum for manufactured spending in the Miles and Points forum at **FlyerTalk.com**.

If you don't want to get into all that, consider working with a family member or friend who needs to make a big purchase and can pay you back. You can also time your credit card applications with big purchases you have to make. If you can't meet the minimum for the spending bonus, don't get the card!

ACHTUNG! Manufactured spending involves creating purchases that will equate to points and miles, especially to hit introductory bonuses. For example: using your credit card to buy a gift card for a store you plan to spend at anyway. It's legal, but it can be seen as a dubious spending practice because similar activities are used for illegal activities. **TheFrequentMiler.com** will give you an overview on keeping it legal (which, yes, is what you should do).

EfN: What is "churning"?

Churning is when you sign up for credit cards, earn the bonus points, then cancel the cards before paying any of the associated card fees. There are different rules against churning to prevent consumers from doing it repeatedly. For example, at the time of writing, Chase [Bank] won't approve you for a new card if you have opened five or more within the past two years.

EfN: Why do you think more people don't use travel hacking?

It can be a bit scary to deal with things like multiple credit cards. I think it's best to get involved on whatever level feels comfortable for you. You can be ultra-conservative and use only one card and still earn free travel.

EfN: Who shouldn't get involved with travel hacking?

Again, those who can't responsibly manage credit cards or have credit card debt. It's just a bad idea.

EfN: But seriously, how will applying for all these credit cards not hurt my credit score?

It will ding your score for a short period of time, but then it bounces back; many say it actually increases their score after a short hit. If you think about it, it makes sense. The score is basically a way to tell if you pay your debts. When you take on more credit cards and debts and always pay everything back on time, you are earning more trust as someone who pays their debts. That idea is what the score reflects.

EfN: One of the biggest mental barriers to getting involved in travel hacking is the idea of managing all those credit cards. Do you have any advice on making this work?

If you are responsible with a credit card right now, you'll be fine. But if getting one or multiple credit cards makes you nervous, don't do it. Do what feels comfortable and right for you.

 TECH TIP: Hey—there's technology for that! Use a spreadsheet or calendar to create your own structure, or web-search "spreadsheet to track multiple credit cards" to find a template or app.

EfN: What are your pointers to finding a rewards card?

Right now, Chase Bank has the best deals—you can check directly on their site. If you want to see the latest offers, check sites like **ZerotoTravel.com**, **ExtraPackofPeanuts.com**, and **ThePointsGuy.com**

EfN: Let's talk perks. There are accommodations, flights, general points, and other types. In what direction would you steer the budget traveler?

It depends on your goals. I think as far as credit cards are concerned, flights will allow you to save the most money as long as you use the points properly. Each credit card has its own unique rules. For example, as of writing, Chase allows you to earn "Chase Points," but you can transfer those points and turn them into United Airlines miles to book through United.com. There are many types of microstrategies like that that allow you to maximize your points.

EfN: Do you have any favorite perks?

Having the ability to fly cheaply nearly anywhere. It's awesome! For example, right now I have 165,000 Chase points. I could book a round-trip flight anywhere in the world and, with taxes and fees, most likely pay under $100. That's insane! Or I could fly in style in business class. It's so nice to have that type of flexibility.

EfN: Do you have a specific process for scoring rewards cards, or do you simply keep an eye on good deals when you know you have a trip or big expense coming up?

I've got my core cards now and don't mess too much with getting new cards. It really comes down to the offer, the minimum spend, plus fees. The way points can be redeemed varies from card to card, but generally speaking, anything 50,000 points or higher is pretty solid. There are other factors too. If your airport is a hub for a particular airline, it might make sense to just get cards with that airline. Or, if you are only traveling around the US, go for Southwest points. It depends on your situation.

EfN: Is there an advisable length of time to hold onto miles or rewards?

Use them when you need them and when you have them. You never know when an airline or hotel will decide to devalue your points.

ACHTUNG! Did you catch what he said there? Your points might be DEVALUED after a certain amount of time. Did I say "read the fine print" yet?

EfN: Any consistent top picks among rewards cards?

Chase Sapphire Preferred and the Chase business cards are excellent. Anything with United is solid, because they have the most flexibility when it comes to using your points.

EfN: Are there certain types of rewards cards that you specifically do not recommend?

I personally don't like anything around Delta. They make it difficult to use points, plus I don't usually fly them.

EfN: Is there a certain application process you would recommend or anything else to keep in mind before or during applying?

My buddy Travis from **Extra Pack of Peanuts** introduced me to what he calls the "app-o-rama." Basically, you apply for new credit cards all at once and diversify, say, five applications across three different banks. Since each credit card is going to ping your credit report, doing it at the same time makes it less likely there will be any red flags because it's happening all at once. Therefore, you'll have a better chance of getting approved for all the cards. Plus, if you get them all on the same date, it's easy to remember when to cancel.

I've done this once. It was fun (well, as fun as filling out credit card applications can be), but I probably won't do it again because I'm happy with my core set of cards. If you are going to get multiple cards anyway, this is a good strategy.

EfN: Finally, tell us about one of your favorite travel hacking experiences.

I'm from the US and was dating a Norwegian girl I met in Brazil, but being 4,000 miles apart made things a bit difficult! I upped my travel hacking game for love and flew to Norway multiple times for under $50. That felt damn good and made the relationship possible. Now we are married! The moral? Travel hacking will lead you to your soulmate and destiny. Okay, that is total crap, but you will be able to get some crazy cheap flights.

Thanks, Jason!

With Jason Moore's expert tutelage, you've now completed Travel Hacking 101. There are a few final travel hacking tips to keep in mind once you get the process started:

⇨ Points and miles are still money, they just have different names and values. Avoid becoming an overnight big spender—work to find good deals! 40,000 miles can be put toward a flight ticket, but find a cheap seat—*yes*, avoid business class—and you'll have miles to spare.

⇨ *Never* miss out on a bonus deadline after signing up.

⇨ Points and miles don't always mean bookings, especially if what you're after (e.g., a popular flight route or hotel) is in high demand. So, plan ahead and be flexible.

⇨ If your card application is declined, call and request a manual review. Systems are often automated, and you may find more leniency with a real person.

⇨ If you want to delve further, **NerdWallet.com** has an excellent breakdown of travel hacking, credit score relation, and rewards program comparisons.

⇨ Search online for company restrictions for the card you're considering. Chase, for example, may not approve applications for certain cards if the person has applied for five or more cards within the preceding 24 months.

⇨ Chase Sapphire, Charles Schwab Debit, and MasterCard Cash Passport are all great travel cards with which you can kick off your research. Outside of the US, search online for the best cards in your country.

Chapter 6: Standard Airfare Booking

Learning the ins and outs of the airline industry will not only help you maximize miles and points from travel hacking, it will also save you hundreds to thousands on standard ticket purchases. All that money you save can go straight to more mangoes on a tiny island in Peru or views of Milan from atop its ancient Duomo cathedral.

Don't be a newb and purchase an expensive plane ticket in one sitting just because it's easier and it "saves you time." Fine, yes—it *does* save you time, and time *is* money. But you lost hundreds of dollars in possible savings in order to save, what, 30 total minutes of research (that you can spread out over a couple months?!). I don't exactly call that getting paid for that time you "saved."

If you're less than interested in spending time understanding flight price fluctuations, consider this:

Say you're planning a trip abroad to begin in four months. If I offer you $300 cash-in-hand to spend five minutes every day for three weeks researching your route's airfare, would you do it? That's over $170 an hour—pretty good, right? Not researching airfare often means giving up at *least* that much dough. Just because the money isn't in your hand now doesn't mean it won't be. It's future money, but it's *your* future money.

Convinced? Good.

Now, there are **four main airfare options**. The right one for you completely depends on your personal desires or itinerary, but here's an overview:

1. Round-trip: This most common type of ticket purchase is usually the cheapest and easiest to find and book.

2. Airpasses: These segmented tickets to multiple cities within a region—purchased all at once rather than bit-by-bit—benefit airlines, because it ensures upfront that you'll stick with *their* airline. Airpasses make itineraries less flexible, but if that's not a problem, it's possible to find great deals. Get more information with a search at SmarterTravel.com and BudgetTravel.com.

3. Round-the-World (RTW): These tickets may be up your alley if you wish to travel through multiple continents. There's plenty of flexibility because apart from the first leg, you typically don't need to book tickets far in advance. Considerations vary immensely depending on your ideal route. Visit SmarterTravel.com and search "Around-the-World" to get started.

4. Open-Jaw: These fares allow you to fly from point A to B, then from a *different* destination, C, back to A. Even if a round-trip fare (A→B, B→A) is cheaper, you could lose those savings on travel expenses getting back to B if you've strayed far (to C, for example) during your travels. Visit SmarterTravel.com to better understand if open-jaw fares are right for you.

> **KEEP YO' MONEY:** Always search for single tickets. Grouped tickets will reflect the price of the highest seat within the seating arrangement. Opt instead to pick your seats during the checkout process, or save a few hundred and sit apart.

Finding the Sweet Spot

Once you get an idea of the ticket type that's right for you, start chasing the best fare. Set up price alerts on flight-scanning sites like **Skyscanner.com**, **Kayak.com**, and **Airfarewatchdog.com** (my current favorites), and allow them to alert you when there's a change in price. This inbox-filling step will help you make sense of the oft fluctuating numbers.

Things looking depressing? Search online for "map of airports in [country name]" to ensure you're not missing out on an overall cheaper option to a nearby airport. Or, try this: Run searches for separate legs of the flight. For example, a flight from Atlanta to Singapore that connects in Los Angeles might be more expensive than purchasing a ticket from Atlanta → Los Angeles, then Los Angeles → Singapore. You can even spend a few days in the stopover city as a bonus!

> **TECH TIP:** Many sites use cookies to track the routes you search, then raise the price each time you look (or after a certain amount of time has elapsed) to pressure you into purchasing. Outsmart them! Prevent tracking by clearing your cookie cache after browsing or by using incognito windows (ctrl+shift+n on PC, cmd+shift+n on Mac). But remember: you can't re-open closed windows or access browser history in incognito mode or after you've cleared your cache.

Next, find sites that notify users of deals, then follow them on social media and sign up for their email lists. Flight-scanning sites often provide the cheapest available fares, but sometimes they don't catch special discounts or promotions offered by the airlines. Certain airlines (like Southwest, JetBlue, RyanAir, Vueling, and other small or new companies) may also be omitted. One of my favorite companies for deals is **ScottsCheapFlights.com**, but here are a few more:

⇨ TheFlightDeal.com

⇨ Airfarewatchdog.com

⇨ Skiplagged.com

⇨ ThePointsGuy.com

⇨ @FlyerTalkMileageRuns

⇨ SecretFlying.com

⇨ Hipmunk.com

⇨ Momondo.com (especially for international trips.)

⇨ GoEuro.com for European destinations (this site also looks at trains and buses.)

⇨ HolidayPirates.com

⇨ Kiwi.com

Google's ITA Matrix often (but beware—not always!) finds the cheapest routes, though I prefer to use it just for an overview of available options. You can't buy tickets on it, though, so it's just a launching point.

Check as many of those sites as possible, because results vary nearly every time. Oh, and begrudgingly remember that the price you see first is typically not the final price. Carefully review charges for taxes and additional fees (like baggage) before getting too excited.

 KEEP YO' MONEY: Another benefit to signing up for deal-scanning sites is that they catch *mistake fares.* Sometimes airlines accidentally list flights at *hundreds* of dollars below cost. Until they catch and correct the mistake, they have to honor the bookings made with the incorrectly listed price!

Finally, sign up for email newsletters from the airlines themselves for special deals only sent out through email. Get started at Airfarewatchdog for my favorite lists of US domestic and international airlines.

 TECH TIP: Some flight aggregation websites price-discriminate based on location with the excuse that certain country denizens will pay more than others. For example, **Skyscanner.cz** (Czech Republic) might show cheaper prices than **Skyscanner.com** (US).

When it comes to booking, some experts say there are simply *no* trends behind prices and timing, but others disagree. I'm siding with the dissenters—if nothing else, we've all seen how flights are usually more expensive as the departure date approaches. Still, having flexible dates greatly increases your odds of cheap routes—most search engines have an option for this. Here are some useful timing queries and the results I've garnered over the years. Still, I urge you to always check online for industry changes (my go-to is FareCompare.com).

Search Engine Queries to Help Along the Way

⇨ **"Best day to purchase airline tickets"**
 - A broad query for a pricing overview
 - Not the same thing as querying the best day to *fly*

- Cheapest reported to be found on Tuesday, Wednesday, or Saturday
- Highest prices usually found on Friday and Sunday
- Expand with "best day to book flights in [country name]"

⇨ **"Best day to fly" and "Best time of day to fly"**

- Not the same thing as querying the best day to *purchase*
- Fewer flights are booked for Tuesdays, Wednesdays, and Saturdays, plus very early or late in the day. Following supply and demand, fares tend to be cheaper during these times.

⇨ **"Best time to travel to/from [country name]"**

- Get an overall picture of your destination's flight situation. Are there off-season deals? Holy days or holidays? Tourist-heavy periods when prices surge?
- If you need to fly on costlier days, look for cheap flights into a nearby city's airport and take a cheaper train, bus, or car to your primary destination.

⇨ **"How far in advance to book flights to [country name]?"**

- Results vary depending on the country and type of travel (international, national, or regional).
- International flights are usually cheaper when arranged two to three months in advance.
- National and regional flights are usually better to book one to two months in advance.

⇨ **"Best day to book flights from [country A] to [country B]"**

- Check for any other useful information about your route. You might have less luck here, but it's worth a shot!

⇨ **"Best days to book flights on [X] airlines"**

- Not always fruitful, but sometimes it pays off!

⇨ **"Small/budget airlines that fly into [country/city name]"**

- Most flight-aggregation websites don't include new, small, or otherwise outlier airlines. Check the airport website to see which airlines fly there. Each aggregation website should have a list of the airlines they include, so check to see if any are missing.

Some queries have specific answers and some will be fruitless. Think of finding the best fare as a sport—become a skilled player! No game is ever fully predictable, but the better athlete you are, the higher your odds of winning.

Boost the Odds: Bonus Tips and Reminders

⇨ Track Historical Data: Use FareDetective.com or Hopper.com to track your route's pricing over the past few years and get a baseline pricing idea.

⇨ Check GoEuro.com for European destinations. This site also looks at trains and buses.

⇨ Consider booking on websites with a price match guarantee (Expedia, American Airlines, Ebookers, Priceline, and Yapta, to name a few). Don't forget to check for lower prices later on. Your browser might have an add-on or extension to notify you of cheaper fares *while* you're searching—InvisibleHand is one option.

⇨ Bidding websites like Hotwire.com and Priceline.com can score you great deals. Want a better idea of what the score will be? Search online for information others have posted about their own bid history—start at BiddingTraveler.com.

⇨ If you have a close friend or family member who works in the travel industry, consider *politely* asking if they have any buddy passes or coupons that you might purchase with money or infinite high fives. Rules surrounding these passes are strict, so make sure you respect them.

⇨ Upon check-in, find out the cost to upgrade. Sometimes the price of free movies, food, and checked baggage is comparable to what you would have to pay for those extras otherwise!

⇨ Smaller airlines—especially those based in second or third world countries—may be less reliable. Some don't offer refunds even when they cancel the flight! Others could be complete scams from the start. It pays to research questionable companies for reviews and cancellation policies.

⇨ Pack light—obscene fees for checked or oversized luggage are now the norm.

⇨ Check the airport's ACTUAL location; misleading names might lead you to believe it's closer to your final destination than it actually is. For example, Ryanair lists London Stansted as their "London" arrival option. In reality, it's 45 minutes away from London—yet another transport expense. Ew.

⇨ Cheap tickets for frequently run regional routes often have the same price no matter when you book. For example, in Peru you can take a $20, 15-hour bus ride from Lima to Arequipa, or a $50, 2-hour flight purchased same day. I know where I would land! (See what I did there?)

⇨ Never exchange currency in airports—the exchange rate is often grossly inflated.

⇨ Research "airport to [your destination]" transportation in advance to prevent running around like a headless chicken trying to figure out (often in a foreign language) whether to take a bus, train, taxi, or rideshare.

⇨ Food is overpriced at travel terminals, so (being mindful of border crossing rules) try to pack your own food. See Chapter 17 for great portable options.

⇨ Before booking your ticket, ensure you'll have all necessary documents and certifications for entry to a country: visas, proof of vaccinations, a foreign driver's licence, etc.

 TALES FROM THE ROAD: One flight required that I arrive in Milan's Malpensa Airport at 6 a.m. Public transportation didn't run that early and a taxi would cost $90. My solution? The night before my flight, I hit **the famous aperitivo scene** in town (free food with happy hour drinks), then that same night at 11 p.m., I took the last $14 train to the airport. Once checked-in, my supply of ear plugs and a yoga-mat-cum-sleeping-pad constructed between two fake plants gave me five hours of rest before boarding time.

Don't get me wrong, I love sleep—I'm a zombie with anything fewer than six hours—so I suggest airport-camping only if you have a comfy place to lie down, a good set of earplugs, and an eye mask (which can just be a sock or hat). It's not the best sleep of your life, but think of it this way:

Opting for the train and less sleep instead of the taxi was like earning $15 an hour.

$90 taxi - $14 train = $76 in savings
$76 in savings ÷ 5 hours of vague discomfort = $15 per hour!

$15 extra dollars per hour sounds like adventure money to me!

Interlude:
Dan and the Van / East Ireland

"Let's wrap Frankie up in the garden hose!"

Dot, all freckles and excitement, is attempting with strange affection to torment her little brother.

"Do it, do it!!" Frankie yells enthusiastically.

Being the two adults in the situation, Mr. Jams and I fetch the hose. Our adult status also confers the requisite strength to coil the hose around Frankie's flailing body and roll him across the Irish green summer grass. In no time, he's utterly tangled. His toothless mouth laughs maniacally while Dot jumps for joy at her sibling's incapacitation. Why is this so fun?

First and foremost, please don't mistake me for someone who's kid crazy—I'm not. I seldom opt to spend time with other humans at all. Maybe the exception here is simply that these two are gingers like me. Maybe it's that Dot's smile has a sweetness and wisdom stretching far beyond her 13 years. Or that Frankie—once he works through crippling shyness—is so full of impish 11-year-old playfulness that it's impossible not to want to make mischief with him.

I have a feeling that despite the many things I'll miss about 16 months of work-exchange—the landscape of Italy, the food of Turkey, the relaxation of Greece—no pang of nostalgia will hit harder than when my thoughts rest upon scenes of giggling Frankie and Dot.

They get their playfulness from their father. When Dan unfolded his imposing 6'3" frame out of the van to pick me up at the train station, I was duped into thinking he was a serious man (his silver-toned hair and pinched, stern expression were also part of the ruse), but I was wrong.

Mr. Jams and I have almost as much fun with Dan as we do Frankie and Dot. His dry Irish wit meshes well with our humor, and it's nice to connect in English—even better with an Irish brogue mixed in. Work-exchange means almost constant interaction with foreign language speakers, which can be tiresome for hosts and volunteers alike.

As the minority gender in the house, I suspect that both Dan and Frankie find in my beau a masculine reprieve from the primarily female cadre of volunteers. Margaret, Dan's wife, is a masterful chef and baker, and the home's breadwinner. As such, their work-exchange is primarily kitchen production and tends to attract women.

Six days a week, Margaret is in the kitchen by 4 a.m. and stays until it's time to prepare dinner for her family and the volunteers. Dan logs almost as much time as the resident chauffeur. At any given moment, he's probably ferrying volunteer arrivals and departures to and from the train station or the cafe they run, shuttling Frankie and Dot to school and extracurriculars, delivering food across the region to restock cafes and restaurants, or collecting payments for their sales.

This all takes place in the home's only vehicle—the big yellow "delivery" van. Seeing in Mr. Jams the chance to have a chauffeur protégé, Dan decides to teach him the winding routes of the countryside.

Dan, Mr. Jams, and I sit in a row on the van's drab gray front seat that stretches door-to-door (I simply lucked out as the defacto girlfriend-copilot) and careen through the emerald-green Irish hills to learn Dan's routes. To pass the time, he recounts stories from 20 years spent as an apprentice in his sister's alteration shop, or we sing along to classic rock and tell whatever crude jokes we can remember.

Once Dan feels confident in Mr. Jams' driving ability, he washes his hands of the endless shuttling about. It will be back to chauffeuring when our work-exchange ends, but he intends to enjoy this taste of van-less freedom while he can. We don't complain—as far as work-exchange options go, casually driving around Ireland is cream of the crop!

It is a hot summer in July and the sunniest one Ireland has seen in nearly two decades. Between deliveries, we visit nearby tourist sites like the ruins of 11th century Cahir Castle and the Woodstock Gardens & Arboretum. One sweltering day, we take Frankie and Dot to swim in nearby River Suir. Immediately following four near-perfect cannonball entries, we notice a large escaped hog lounging nearby on the other side of the river. We keep swimming, of course.

If all that action isn't enough, my late-July birthday rolls around and Mr. Jams presents me tickets to a Bruce Springsteen concert. The Boss is playing in nearby Kilkenny, about 30 minutes away, so the van is crucial to getting there and staying late into the night after the buses have stopped running.

But there's a hitch: several of the other volunteers want in on the van action. Our home base is a town without nightlife, so the volunteers conspire to use Mr. Jams' driving for a riotous night in Kilkenny while we rock out to New Jersey music royalty.

But full stop. The van seats only three, and it's illegal to have more than that in the vehicle. Once in a while, if an extra passenger needs a quick lift, they'll climb onto the cool metal floor of the van's refrigerated back compartment. It's been gutted and closed off from the front. It's dark, cramped, and cold, and when the big door slides shut, those daring passengers are encased in a windowless pitch black. They listen for the engine to start, and the ride begins.

Save for the constant potholes and snake-like twists in the roads, it is as near to a sensory deprivation chamber as you can imagine. It's also a ton of fun! And convenient! But still illegal.

Nonetheless, Margaret and Dan agree to let us take the others in the van as long as we are "safe." To Kilkenny we go—not three, not four, but eight!

The next Saturday arrives, and predicting a night of debauchery, Mr. Jams does not want to drive a vanload of tipsy foreigners 30 minutes back through the country roads at two in the morning. We devise a plan.

Noting that four properly positioned people can lie flat in the back of the van and two more can rest in the front, six "beds" are accounted for. The remaining two? They'll camp—we have a tent!

Legality isn't the issue here, *success* is. So, with three stuffed side by side in the front and five tucked into the darkness of the van's bed, we set off over the Irish hills. What can possibly go wrong?

We want to be within walking distance of the festivities, but we also need the van strategically situated to hide the tent. The basic idea is to leave space between the front of the van and the top edge of a wall-abutting parking space. Within the six feet of relatively hidden space between van and abutment, we'll surreptitiously mount our tent.

But upon pulling into the city center's public parking lot, we quickly deduce that our prospects are grim. Driving the behemoth van through the narrow parking lanes, it becomes apparent that finding a space to suit our needs is highly unlikely. The only abutments we see are against other parked cars or the whizzing main road.

As we meander toward the exit, we see it: an empty spot facing a short stretch of vine-covered stone wall. Creeping forward, Mr. Jams pulls the van in just far enough so as not to block the thoroughfare. With the sun still shining, we decide that saving the tent setup for later will increase our odds of remaining unnoticed.

Until then, the night is ours! Representing France (Jean, 24); Spain (Jose, 23, and Maria, 33); China (Han, 48); Switzerland (Annette, 25); Germany (Franzi, 28); and the US (Mr. Jams and myself), we hit the town running.

Stumbling back to ol' Big Yellow in the wee hours of the night, we find the parking lot mostly empty. Despite the lack of additional coverage from adjacent cars, we decide the coast is as clear as it's going to get. The following Sunday's daybreak should be lazy enough that we can discreetly pack up and hit the road at dawn. Mr. Jams and I don our headlamps and get to work on the tent.

Falling asleep comes surprisingly easily, and the next morning I slide the van's side door open to greet four groggy faces rising from the deep sleep they'd found inside. We pack up while munching on baked inventory we'd pilfered (with permission) from Margaret's bakery. Our heroic driver takes a deep breath as he slides behind the wheel and we bounce back, illegally, to a new day's work in our sleepy small town.

⚓ Chapter 7: Road Master

Throughout my 20s, I figured car rental was something I'd only be able to do once I "grew up" and earned "real money" (whatever that means). Well, I was wrong. Using a car on your travels can actually be done more cheaply than using a car any other time.

Some credit cards offer points toward car rentals, but if you aren't using a rewards program, you're still in luck! While there are many ways to cut costs in traditional renting, we'll soon discuss the game changer to make it *free* … but first, a primer on a concept you haven't heard since first grade: carpooling!

Carpooling

America is catching up to the rest of the world when it comes to carpooling, the unsung hero of budget travel. It's not just for caffeine-deprived moms and dads, or suburban train-shy commuters. Drivers worldwide have embraced carpooling websites for years to quickly connect with all sorts of traveling and commuting passengers. Usually, each passenger pays a fee to offset auto and related expenses like gas mileage, tolls, even sometimes wear and tear maintenance!

Whether you're a driver or passenger, sharing rides is a stellar way to meet kindred travelers or knowledgeable locals while traveling comfortably (and saving heaps of cash). Using carpool websites, drivers post their routes anywhere from hours to months in advance, and they'll include how far off-route they'll go for pick-ups and drop-offs. Also detailed are the number of seats available and the cost per seat.

To start registration on any popular carpool websites in your country, create a well-written, detailed profile to give drivers a good idea of what it would be like spending time in a car with you. Most websites walk you through this process.

Be candid about your personality and ride style to increase the odds of carpooling with a compatible group. List your preferences regarding smoking, idle chitchat, bladder-break requirements, and even music. There's nothing worse than being stuck in a carpool headed out of Paris with nothing but thrashing Frédéric Leclercq on the stereo when all you wanted was to mellow out with some Stromae! AmIright?!

Once your brilliant carpool profile is set up, post your route if you're a driver (remember to factor in possible toll costs) or search for applicable rides as a passenger. Get creative—some drivers may not be able to take you all the way to your final destination, but they can bring you as close as possible. If you can buy a ticket there, it might save you more money in the end.

Check early and often for newly posted routes. If it's an option, post a "ride needed" ad for the route you're taking so drivers can contact you. In addition to advance communication with possible drivers or passengers, always check their profiles and reviews by other riders to increase the odds of a safe, compatible, and peaceful trip.

Here are some **top carpool websites** per country; but always search online for "carpooling/ridesharing in [country name]" for new arrivals to the online and app scene:

Multiple Country: CarpoolWorld.com, BlaBlaCar.com,
    Jayride.com, Craigslist Rideshare (city specific)
Europe: Karzoo.eu, GoMore.com, Ridefinder.eu
US: GroupCarpool.com, eRideShare.com, Rdvouz.com
Canada: HitchPlanet.com, Kangaride.com
India: Carpooling.in
Brazil: Zazcar.com.br
Chile: Nosfuimos.cl
Japan: Noritomosan.com/en
Russia: Dublway.com
Asia: Rydesharing.com
Australia & New Zealand:
    CoSeats.com (or "co.nz")

ACHTUNG! Always inform a trusted someone else about your route and the driver's full contact information!

Carpooling can be more like a sitcom than any other transportation method, because you're dealing with autonomous, private drivers and passengers. User reviews should help weed out the undesirables, but the potential money savings realized by carpooling are probably worth the risk of an awkward conversation or headache-inducing playlist. Still, it never hurts to have a backup plan, because this autonomy also means that people can flake more easily. Some websites use an escrow system to prevent cancellations, some don't. On the plus side, this means fully booked rides might have last-minute spaces open up!

PRO TIP: Message drivers even if their route is booked and ask them to notify you of cancellations. That way, you'll be first in line to snag the seat as a replacement rider!

Rental-Boosting: The Game Changer

As daunting as it may seem to rent a car abroad, the schtick is pretty global once you overcome language barriers. And there's a reward for your bravery: when you combine rental discount strategies with carpoolers, you can say ciao to financial drain and G'DAY to turning a *profit*: we call this *Rental Boosting* and it's a-mazing!

No matter your route, there's a good chance you'll find interested riders. Even if you've yet to rent a car, post your ideal or intended route on any of the aforementioned carpool websites to gauge interest. At a minimum, you can have your car rental costs covered. Beyond that, it's all profit! Post routes as early as possible—there will be competition among drivers on the popular sites, and riders browsing for less-popular routes usually check less often.

And get this, sometimes you can rent a car for less than a dollar a day. Tack on some paying carpoolers and you can practically fund a whole trip! Transfercarus.com provides *free* one-way relocation rentals for certain routes in the US and Canada. Imoova.com offers similar rentals in Australia, New Zealand, Canada, UK, US, and Europe from a dollar a day! Can you say, "road trip"?!

The freedom to stop and explore wherever the road takes you is hard to beat. And to maintain your budget-conscientiousness, you can save on accommodation by choosing cheaper options that are off the beaten path, especially with rural couchstays or camping. Apart from using carpoolers and alternate accommodation to recoup costs, there are other ways to minimize cash flow that we'll cover below.

 TALES FROM THE ROAD: My sister and I spent two weeks travelling over 800 miles and visiting eight cities across Southern France and Northern Spain. Figuring out bus or train tickets to do this would have used up a lot of precious travel time, and since the trip had a time limit, we opted to pay a bit to expedite getting from place to place. Renting a car, we each ended up paying only $25 a day (including gas). *Zinga!*

Peer-to-Peer (P2P) Car-Sharing

Oh the times they are a-changin' for car rentals. Most countries now allow everyday car owners to rent out their personal cars through insured web services. They cover relevant precautions and provide a central resource to connect car owners with potential renters. It tends to be much cheaper than renting through one of the larger corporate car rental brands.

Search "Car sharing in [country name]" or "Peer car rental in [country name]", or start with the **popular P2P companies** I've listed below:

Europe	UK	US
CarAmigo.eu	HiyaCar.co.uk	Getaround.com
New Zealand	CarClub.Easycar.com	JustShareIt.com
YourDrive.co.nz	Drivy.co.uk	Turo.com
	Australia	
	DriveMyCar.com.au	

Point-to-Point Car Rentals

You may be familiar with urban bike and scooter rentals; thankfully, car companies are following suit. **Car2go.com** and **Zipcar.com** are innovative, low-hassle providers of short-term, temporary rentals. They allow one-way car rentals using an hourly or per-minute rate, atop a minimum flat base fee. Often easily found in downtown parking lots, Zipcar is typically better for longer trips and Car2go for shorter. Most of them are mobile-app enabled, so check your app store or their websites to see where they serve and decide which one works for you.

 INSIDER INFO: Similar app-based electric moped rentals like **Muving.com** in Atlanta, GA, are slowly making their way across the world. Check online to see if one has popped up in your city!

Boost the Odds: Bonus Tips and Reminders

⇨ Small cars are usually cheaper.

⇨ A SIM card with mobile data is usually cheaper than paying for in-car GPS. Either way, I strongly recommend GPS!

⇨ Renting locally or online is often cheaper than at a travel hub like an airport.

⇨ If you use a credit card to book the rental, it may include rental insurance, so make sure you're not paying double for insurance offered by the rental company.

⇨ Rentals typically cover only one registered driver. Charges are steep for breaking the rules—beware!

⇨ ALWAYS fill the gas tank before returning the car; it's way cheaper!

⇨ Don't forget about toll costs! Do your research prior to renting a car—they can get pretty extreme! Websearch "toll price calculator in [country name]."

⇨ Check online for rental company coupons.

⇨ Inventory at rental sites often changes last-minute. Before you're handed the keys, ask for an upgrade at the same price. Why not?

⇨ Try to avoid parking in paid lots. There is usually free or cheap street parking nearby for a few extra minutes of walking. Heck, even if free parking is a mile away, that's only a 15-minute walk and more opportunities to see cool stuff!

⇨ Search "free parking in [city name]" for listings or parking spot finding apps.

⇨ Be *extremely* cautious about signage and check online for translations.

⇨ Driving rules vary from country to country. For example, in France, interstate traffic must yield to oncoming ramp drivers. Study the differences *before* you hit the road! As they say, "Ignorance is no excuse for the law."

Interlude:
The First Hitchhike / Southern France

Mr. Jams and I are flying from America to Montpellier, France. We're kicking off at least a year of travel, and we arrive in France overflowing with naive backpacker optimism. I've haphazardly decided that we'll hitchhike from the airport to our first host, Muriel, a single mother I connected with on Couchsurfing.com.

After our early morning landing, we collect our gigantic backpacks from the baggage carousel. My 40-pound-plus bag implies that I've overpacked on all fronts, yet I forgot to pack blank paper and a marker (rookie mistake). We meander around the terminal sputtering incomprehensible French-sounding "words" to strangers in an attempt to gather supplies.

Finally, a gate agent takes pity upon us, and we craft our masterpiece—it reads: "Vitrolles S. V. P." (shorthand for *s'il vous plaît*, "please" in French). We predict that in no time, we'll be picked up and delivered to our first French dinner and free cozy lodging with a local.

After selling my car months earlier, I'd hitched a few times over the 20-minute mountain pass between Idaho and Wyoming. It was a local route that always felt safe. Now, in a foreign country with strange words and unfamiliar faces, we're attempting to cover 100 miles. We don't speak any French.

Stepping out of the airport, we wistfully watch taxis pass while walking from the passenger loading zone to a patch of grass farther down. We plan to catch someone after a drop-off with hopes that (a) they'll be heading in our intended direction, and (b) they won't mind driving two grinning Americans with backpacks each the size of a compact Peugeot.

We don't know what we're doing, yet it works. After 30 minutes of awkwardly pointing thumbs and bashful (yet hopeful) smiles, a jolly, middle-aged Moroccan woman scoops us up. Mr. Jams and I stifle high fives amid the adrenaline rush, which our driver seems to be sharing. As we try to communicate, the only words we mutually understand are "Big Ben," and that seems to be plenty. Good mojo gets us through any lack of true communication. 30 minutes pass, and she drops us off along a highway on-ramp.

60 miles to go.

Our luck turns.

Speeding cars zoom past, and there's no doubt that Mr. Jams, myself, and our flimsy paper sign are nothing but a blur to drivers. Setting our bags beside the road, we search the shoulder for larger, sturdier sign material. An empty shoebox! That'll do the trick.

The upgrade evinces nary a slow-down. The high-noon heat of Southern France in June keeps us all too aware that we've been thumbing for over an hour. The night before brought only three hours of sleep, so exhaustion, and now hunger and dehydration are beginning to take their toll.

Deciding that our odds of succeeding will be greater if we don't die of heat stroke, I begin looking for a place to nap. A clearing hidden in some shrubbery between the on-ramp and highway seems our best option, and we lug our bags over and unroll our sleeping pads under a canopy of dejection.

Lulled to sleep by the roar of passing trucks and cars, we wake up a couple of hours later surprisingly refreshed, but no more hydrated. After a few bites of the trusty granola I brought along, we get back to work.

Two more uneventful hours pass, and I'm losing faith in the national enthusiasm we were told France has toward hitchhiking. Our feelings of despair peak right around the time another Moroccan named Khalid takes pity upon us. He's a 20-something with choppy English and an athletic build, and he and Mr. Jams "talk" about soccer mostly just by blurting out random soccer players' names.

Khalid can only provide 15 minutes of route progress, so we disembark at another on-ramp prepared for what we now know could be another four hours of waiting. It will be dark in a couple hours, and we're on a highway in an area far from any main city or bus stop. Will we have to camp?

Our worries prove unfounded, though, for a tiny blue coupe arrives after only 20 minutes. Xavier is a young French engineering student who's enthusiastic about getting a chance to practice his English. *Jackpot!* He takes us the remaining 45 minutes to our destination, even though the final 15 miles are out of his way. Our biggest bit of travel magic yet!

We disembark among an isolated smattering of beige condos and find our host, Muriel, smiling in her doorway. She welcomes us in, and we very nearly drool at the site of a basement floor Muriel covered in comfy blankets and cushions.

After much-needed showers, we're granted permission to raid her refrigerator and prepare a home-cooked dinner. Pasta with a lemon-caper mascarpone cream sauce and Muriel's *bagna cauda*, a heavenly anchovy-garlic sauce served with crunchy raw carrots and cauliflower.

Sated by a quality meal, a bottle of Bordeaux, and the comforting company of our host, Mr. Jams and I collapse onto our makeshift blanket palette. We've survived the first day. Who knows how many more are to come?

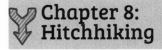

Chapter 8: Hitchhiking

It's the longest-known way to get somewhere for free, and while hitchhiking may not be for everybody, I *do* suggest everybody try it at least once (you know, safely). If you need inspiration, consider the two guys from Beijing that spent three months hitchhiking across 13 countries and nearly 10,000 miles to visit a girlfriend in Berlin.[1] Or how about the Big Bummit, where each year, over a hundred students break into groups of two or three and hitchhike for charity from England to another country (like Lithuania, Poland, or Latvia!)?

Hitchhiking will always have staunch naysayers, but these detractors are often victims of the ever-irrational *negativity bias*, a lovely little concept that helps us humans recall negative events more frequently than positive ones. Think about it: thousands of people worldwide hitchhike

---

[1] http://www.chinahush.com/2010/02/21/beijing-guys-hitch-hike-all-the-way-to-visit-ones-girlfriend-in-berlin/

with success every day, but the negativity bias confirms a tendency to focus on hitchhiking horror stories and Hollywood plotlines. It's like fearing sharks even though you're more likely to be hit by an asteroid or comet than attacked by a shark.[2]

Hitchhiking evokes a true sense of adventure that can only be found on the open road (literally). As with all things, awkward people surface every so often, but for the most part you'll be attracting fellow adventurers. Drivers, too, are facing the same risks as the hitchhikers they pick up; but they're also creating their own mini-adventures by talking to fascinating travelers who have their black belts in the art of free travel! Enjoy each exchange for what it is: a spontaneous meeting of strangers, a chance to learn, and a great story to tell!

> **A HITCHER'S TAKE:** "You will need thick skin. Lots of people will drive past and shout or stare at you like you're insane. I remember once trying to hitch out of a gas station for about an hour then going in to get a drink and a break, and having the clerk talk to me about the 'weird girl outside' not realizing it was me."
>
> - Chel Barnes, nomad extraordinaire

Pre-Road Preparation

Got that thumb primed? Ready to take on this ancient(ish?) travel art that's ecological, adventurous, *and* free?! Then let's talk about the ways to prepare before leaving home.

1. Know the gesture

Is it a thumb or index finger pointed up or down? Back of the hand? A wave? Or even something else? Different countries use different gestures, and using the wrong one could make some drivers very, very angry. In certain Middle East and Asian countries, for example, the American thumbs-up is particularly obscene!

2. Pack food, gear, and homemade sign materials

Think of hitchhiking as a sport: it requires gear—especially for longer distances. Pack plenty of water and food, since the time you'll

---

[2] http://www.tulane.edu/~sanelson/Natural_Disasters/impacts.htm

spend waiting is relatively unpredictable. Some people have to wait days if the area is sparsely populated, so if this is your case, have a tent or backup plan.

Throwing *just* your thumb out is a way to give your fate to the road, but if you have a specific destination, a sign greatly increases pickup odds. Signs eliminate uncertainty for drivers and prevent them from telling themselves you're probably not going in their direction. Find pieces of cardboard before or during your travels and have a thick permanent marker at the ready.

PRO TIP: Learn how to say "please" in the country's language, and write it on your sign. In fact, some are successful by writing just that one phrase! Politeness will get you far in any language.

3. Know where you're going

Hitchhiking is synonymous with going with the flow, but advance planning is useful. First, you need to know if it's safe and legal to hitchhike in the country you're considering. You'll find general warnings against hitching no matter where you go, but in some countries it might be ardently ill-advised, so take heed.

Familiarize yourself with stops along your route. This way, if a driver stops and tells you they're going to a place that isn't your destination, you'll know if it's worth jumping in. Furthermore, if you're aiming to cover long distances, you're more likely to be picked up by requesting stops only 20 to 50 miles away from your starting point. It may mean more stops overall, but think about it: what are the odds of finding someone who happens to be on your exact long-distance route? (Remember to pack enough supplies for multiple homemade signs!)

It also helps to know transportation hub locations along the way in case you want to throw in the towel and hop a bus or train.

4. Meet your new best friend: Hitchwiki.org

This is an indispensable resource during and before your travels. It's a collaborative website and can help you find routes, places to stay, and advice for your plans.

5. Find a prime spot to stand (in advance!)

Don't just stand anywhere; use a strategy. But, safety first! Use online satellite maps to ensure you'll be able to stand as far off the road as possible. You don't need me or YouTube videos to know that drivers can be crazy!

Once you've found your spot, stand where it's easy for drivers to slow down. Stop signs, stop lights, gas stations, and on-ramps are all ideal. Online maps and Hitchwiki are your best bets here.

 INSIDER INFO: Read the legal fine print. For example, in most of the US, it's only illegal to stand literally *on* a roadway to hitchhike. As long as you're off the pavement (or gravel, cobblestone, etc.), it's fair game!

6. Be weather aware

Check the forecast to be ready, but also skip hitchhiking in extremely cold or hot climates unless you feel *supremely* confident that you have the gear, food, and water to risk it.

7. Know about self-defense

Be prepared for a worst-case scenario, however unlikely. Look up the country's emergency phone number, and have it dialed and ready to call. Turn on your phone's GPS so you'll be easier to locate by others. A pen (sorry, eyeballs!) and mace can be good ways to defend yourself. Refrain from knives unless you're skilled, as they can be turned against you.

In general, travelers should know basic self-defense. Know where to hit, how to protect yourself, and how to roll out of a moving car. Better safe than sorry.

Time to Hit the Road

You know where you're going, along with what's safe and legal, and you have your gear packed and ready. Now, let's talk about being a road-wise hitchhiker.

1. Look the part

The rule of first impressions also applies to hitchhikers. You'll be more appealing if you wear a smile and bright clothing (but depending on the country and your gender, dress appropriately). Females should not be scantily clad. Try to appear confident and friendly—that's the type of person most sane drivers will want in their car.

For some real visual appeal, add a touch of humor to your signs. Something like "Free Cookies!" (if you actually have cookies) or "Great Conversationalist!" should do the trick.

2. Keep the most important belongings on your person

In the improbable situation of having to ditch the car without your bag, this precaution is invaluable. Disperse important belongings throughout pockets, travel wallets, boot bottoms, etc.

3. Don't hitch at night

Firstly, low visibility means you could get hit by a vehicle. Secondly, darkness means fewer ways to assess the situation's safety. The same goes for the driver. Why would they pick someone up if they can't see them in all that darkness? Would you?

4. Expect to wait

It could take anywhere from two minutes to two days. A populated area might average out to an hour of wait time (but I'm not making any promises). Common sense will be your best predictor here.

5. Expect bizarre passerby reactions

Some people seem to take hitchhiking personally. Maybe they'll flip you the bird or holler at you out the window. Ignore it. In some cases, you'll get encouraging honks, smiles, and waves!

Ride-Ready

It's exciting to have a car pull over, but don't let excitement blind you to pragmatics and precaution. While you may be tempted to accept whatever driver comes along (especially if you've been waiting a long time), there will always be a place to sleep, and there will always be another ride on the way. Here are some rules for hopping in:

1. Talk to the driver before you (and your bag) get in

Assess creep-factor and whether the driver seems to be under the influence of anything. Slurring, drooping or heavy eyelids, or avoiding eye contact are all big no-nos, so spark up a little conversation to gather information. Trust your gut—it's your most useful travel tool.

If you accept the ride, thank them, and prime them for good behavior by saying something like, "There are so many weirdos out there, I really appreciate you helping me stay safe!"

2. Take a photo of the license plate

Ask the driver if it's okay to take a photo of their license plate and send it to a friend—"No offense," you can add—"Safety first!" If they're not okay with it, politely decline the ride.

3. Keep your bag with you

Never put your bag in a trunk or somewhere inaccessible. You might forget it, or the driver could ride off with it.

4. Sit in front

This isn't a taxi. If the driver requests you sit in the back and the front seat is open, don't take the ride. Sit in front to be better aware of your surroundings and keep a better eye on the driver. Obviously, two can be stronger than one, so if there's a front seat passenger, be extra wary.

5. Be a good passenger

This goes without saying, but I'll say it anyway: the driver isn't your chauffeur. Stay awake! It's rude to fall asleep, but more importantly, stay awake to stay safe and aware.

Also remember that they're doing you a favor, and the favor you pay in return is being a good copilot. Try some innocent chit chat (if that's what they seem to want), and stay away from sensitive subjects (religion, politics, etc.). Maybe they picked you up because they were bored and wanted some company or a distraction. It's a small price to pay.

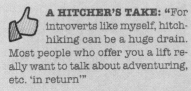

A HITCHER'S TAKE: "For introverts like myself, hitchhiking can be a huge drain. Most people who offer you a lift really want to talk about adventuring, etc. 'in return'"

- Chel Barnes, nomad extraordinaire

6. Go with a friend if it's an option

If you're traveling alone, you can find hitchhiking companions by posting on Facebook, Hitchwiki, or Couchsurfing.com message boards. You may be surprised at how many are up for the adventure.

Michele,
Thank you so much
for reading, &
welcome home!
Hopefully this copy
takes you through
with No BS
thieves!
Happy trails :)
-Meggan

7. Leave if it's awkward

If at *any* point you feel unsafe, get out of the car. Ask to stop because you feel car sick or need to go to the restroom, or just get out at a slow-down or traffic stop. Explanations are not needed. Your safety is far more important than the adventure of hitchhiking.

We've taken care of most safety precautions, but let's not make this too heavy an issue—hitchhiking is pretty darn fun. Your best bet is to use common sense, be prepared, and ALWAYS trust your gut. Drivers are usually just looking to have a lively experience, so reward the risk they've taken by being a good passenger. Be respectful, and make sure you both leave feeling like you've done something amazing. You have!

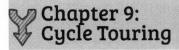

Chapter 9:
Cycle Touring

There are few people I can think of who get me googly-eyed and star-struck. But since we're on the topic, David Bowie (RIP), Michelle Obama, and Rob Greenfield all make the list. Who's that last fellow? Perhaps you don't yet know the name, but there's a reason for that: he intentionally flies under the radar. Self promotion just ain't his thing. Rob's priorities are a bit more profound than those of the average person. Why? Because *he's trying to change the world.*

It is with profound gratitude that I report Rob has teamed up with *Everywhere for Nothing* to help bring free travel to the world. In the end, our overall goals are similar: to make the world a better place. Not only will you soon be exposed to the humble heights at which he lives his life, but also—get ready—you're about to learn the ins-and-outs of free travel through cycle touring from *the man* himself. Even the beginning-est rookie beginners will be ready to hit the road after hearing from Rob.

Self-described as a former "drunk dude" to "dude making a difference," Rob now dedicates his life to uncountable activist and humanitarian issues. He travels the world (six continents and over 40 countries under his belt to date), often (intentionally) penniless, hoping to inspire people to live a more conscientious and sustainable life.

An attempt at summarizing all the good he does is futile, but heck, I'll try anyway. His projects involve bringing awareness to food waste, creating less garbage worldwide, advocating tiny houses and minimalist living, and, of course, promoting sustainable transportation. You can find him on the Discovery Channel, the TEDx stage, YouTube, his website **RobGreenfield.tv**, or his Instagram and Twitter accounts: @RobJGreenfield.

The gist is that Rob is doing whatever he can to lessen the dark side of humanity's impact on earth. At the time of this writing, the number of his possessions hovers around 100. Part of his grand mission involves creating as small of an ecological footprint as possible, so in the realm of travel and transportation, what better tool than the emission-free bike?

Simply by doing his thang, Rob has become a guru on cycle touring. He doesn't just talk the talk, he walks the walk (and bikes the bike). For example, he's biked across America three times, in fewer than four months each time. One was an off-grid ride of 4,700 miles, the others were 4,000 miles and 3,700 miles. That's 12,400 miles of cycling!

The outright adventurous wonder of these trips is drool-worthy, but their true goal is bringing awareness to being better stewards of the earth. So maybe you're saying, "But Meggan, I'm not *trying* to be a better steward of the earth! I just want to travel for free as hedonistically as possible!" Well … that's fine. It's not *really* fine, but also: cycle touring is about as free as it gets. So there's that.

Everybody wins!

The What and How From Rob Greenfield, Eco-Adventurer

EfN: How would you describe cycle touring to the complete newbie?

Cycle touring is pretty simple. It's just using the bicycle as your primary form of transportation. Some people backpack, hitchhike, fly, take buses, or use trains. Cycle touring is a means to adventure and often the adventure itself.

It's also something else: *freedom*—especially from being glued to screens. You're able to get up and go whenever you want. Everything you're traveling with fits right on your bicycle. Since you're in control of your transportation, you don't have to pay to get around. You just hop on your bike and go.

You're getting great exercise and breathing fresh air, and you're not crammed into a space with a bunch of other passengers. Instead, you're exploring the great unknown on your bicycle, and because you have to venture into places most people don't go, it results in some of the most authentic scenarios you can imagine.

EfN: Why do you recommend cycle touring?

The first thing that comes to mind is money—long-term travel is simply so much more accessible to more people since the costs are so minimal. There's the freedom I mentioned before, but it's also exposure to different ways of life. The typical traveler will get a ride or flight from place to place, but on a bicycle, you have no choice but to get outside and immerse yourself in the real world.

Ultimately, it's a challenge that changes your life and almost always for the better. For example, the idea of biking across the US is pretty hard to fathom, but once you've done it, the "big" challenges you might've had to deal with in the past become little speed bumps.

Whatever figurative mountains you come across after a big cycle tour, well, they're just speed bumps, too. You've already biked thousands of miles fueled by sheer willpower—what can hold you back after that? The "challenge" of cycle touring sets up everything else in your life to be easier.

EfN: What is your overall preferred travel method?

Definitely by bicycle, but even better if it's a bicycle and train combo. That way, you can hop on the train and bring your bicycle with you.

EfN: Is there a best type of person for cycle touring?

A lot of people's first answer might be, "young, fit people." That's just not the case. Bicycle touring isn't for any one kind of person. It *is* for anyone who is pursuing an adventure. No question about that. But not an adventure that can only be done by "adventure" people; it's an adventure that can be done by nearly anyone.

The key in a cycle tour is to go at your own pace. Some people like to go 100 miles a day, some people might go just 30. As long as you take it at your own pace, it's accessible to just about everyone. The funny thing is I don't even consider myself a cyclist, even having biked over 15,000 miles and across the country three times. I just consider myself a human being, and I bike.

EfN: Would you recommend cycle touring to someone who feels it's physically beyond them?

I recently did a bike tour across the country for the third time, but this time, 48 people from all walks of life joined. The youngest was around 18 and the oldest was 67. There were women and men from *seven* countries. Most of them never thought they'd do something like that, but now they've cycled across an entire country and their lives are changed forever because of it. If anything, that's the perfect example of how cycle touring is for everyone.

People really underestimate the power of the bicycle. Even I used to. I didn't begin riding until about six years ago when I was 25. It wasn't my own actions that taught me but the people I met over time: a 70-year-old woman biking across the country, 10-year-olds biking alone two miles each way to school, people who seemed 100 pounds overweight biking to work every day. Things like that. As simple as it is, it really is one of the most powerful tools of movement and physical progress that's ever been created by the human race.

EfN: What are some common but mostly unrealistic fears about cycle touring?

A big one is that it's especially dangerous. It's important to take a step back and say, "What *is* dangerous?" versus "What is *perceived* as dangerous?"

The reality is that cycle touring is not a really dangerous thing as far as cycling death goes—more people die per year in cars than on bikes. If people are afraid of a cycling tour because of death risks, well, those risks are inherent (and perhaps *more* risky) in basically any road traveling, so it's a moot point unless you never want to leave the house.

The other dangerous things in life—the big killers—are unhealthy diets and daily stress. Cycle touring naturally helps take care of both those things. It's a low-stress activity, it's physical exercise, and it's easy to eat healthy on the road—especially since you burn so many calories in the process.

EfN: What's something most people don't know about cycle touring?

What you find on the road is that people out there are amazing. You meet the nicest people. When non-cyclers find out what you're doing—"You're biking from *where* to *where*??"—they are always so amazed, and they want to be a part of your adventure. Basically, they want to help you! When you're at a restaurant and you meet a stranger, they may buy your lunch. Often, you'll be riding down the road late in the day and people drive by, slow down, and ask, "What are you doing?" And after you tell them, they say, "Need a place to sleep tonight? I live up the road." People turn out to be incredibly generous to touring cyclists.

EfN: How easy or difficult is it to play tourist while on the road?

Cycle touring is perfect for playing tourist! You just ride your bike right up to the places you want to see and ride on. You might have to find a place to store your stuff, but you can probably leave it wherever you're staying if you find a host through one of the online options I'll mention soon. Even if you're not staying with a host overnight, you can contact them about keeping your belongings safe for you.

EfN: What are important mental preparations for and during a cycle tour?

Take it one pedal, one mile, and one day at a time. Often, looking ahead at how far you still have to go can be overwhelming. If you just take it one thing at a time, you set small goals and ensure continued success. When I'm having a hard time, I count my pedals because I know about how many pedals are in a mile. That's my motivation, and as I continue doing it I think, "Wow! Another mile ... another mile ... another mile!" Just pay attention to your body and what feels right. If one day you're exhausted and you just can't go another mile, then that can be it for the day. That's the freedom of cycle touring—you simply stop when you need to.

EfN: What are common pitfalls and ways to avoid them?

One of the biggest is simply not being prepared. Because you grow so dependent upon the bicycle during a tour, a mechanical breakdown can often lead to a sort of mental breakdown. The thing is, nearly every mechanical breakdown can be prevented with preparedness. For example, a person might ride for too long on bald tires, getting flat after flat, and finally they can't fix a flat and get stuck somewhere. But if they had carried a spare tire, they could've fixed and avoided that problem. As a minimalist, I try to carry as little as possible, but on a bike tour you want to carry the basic and necessary gear—especially spare parts that will prevent you from getting stuck. It'll save you a *lot* of trouble.

Preparation is key, but cycle touring *is* a fairly simple thing we're talking about. For my very first trip across the country, I only got my bike two days before I left. I got some gear and necessary replacement parts and I just started.

If you're starting out in "civilization," there are bike shops all over the place and you can often get what you need on the road. We'll talk soon about my essential packing list, which is on the minimalist side.

EfN: How can we wrap our brains around packing!?

Storage: My first bike trip across the country I pulled a small trailer, because often the idea is to have plenty of space for your gear. But I've come to recommend panniers (like saddle bags) instead of trailers, because the more space you have, the more stuff you accumulate, and the harder it is to ride. Unless there's some special reason, like trying to raise awareness about an issue that requires extra supplies, there's usually no need for the additional space.

I began my second bike trip with four panniers—two on the front, two on the back. After 500 miles, I got rid of the two on the front. The less I have, the more I'm able to just enjoy riding. Plus, it's just easier.

Bike: Make sure you get a bike that fits you comfortably based on height and weight. Although, I know people who have done thousands of miles on beach cruisers! If you want a guaranteed good quality bike, the Surly Long Haul Trucker is a go-to. I've never heard of anyone who wasn't happy with that bike, and it's the least likely to have problems.

Essential Gear: *On* the bike, you need a headlight and taillight. Then, you'll usually want a rack and panniers holding a variation of the following smaller items:

⇨ Multi-tool
⇨ Hand pump
⇨ Bare inner tubes
⇨ Chain lube
⇨ Tire levers
⇨ Patch kit for patching tubes
⇨ Helmet

⇨ Spare tires
⇨ Headlamp
⇨ Toothbrush, toothpaste, floss
⇨ Soap
⇨ Sunscreen
⇨ Water and food

Then come the tent, sleeping pad, and sleeping bag. Even if you plan on staying with people or in paid accommodation, you just never know when you might have to set up camp unexpectedly.

An optional but useful item is a solar panel hitch to charge up small devices (headlamps, bike lights, etc.). Apart from that, I advise keeping things minimalist upon setting out. You can usually find a way to get anything else you might need while on the road.

Food: With all that physical exertion, you nearly always have to carry food along. I suggest a little camp stove, reusable plates (so you don't create trash), reusable water bottles, carry containers like reusable bags and tupperware. This way when you go somewhere that sells bulk items or a farmers market, you can just fill up the containers you already have. Along with this, a water purifier is great for when you pass rivers and lakes.

Clothing: You don't need anything fancy or specific for cycle touring. I have one pair of very comfortable bike shorts that help cushion my butt from being on the seat for so long. I recommend them, but they're not mandatory. You want the basics depending on climate: rain jacket, outerwear, shirts, pants, and shorts. Most people carry too much clothing and don't need it; they either end up regretting it or toting more weight around than they need. You can always just wash it by hand and let it air dry.

EfN: Can you talk about financing? What's the minimum budget?

Maintenance and Startup: The main costs are food, the bike itself, parts, and accommodation. If you're racking up thousands of miles, you'll just need new parts, plain and simple. New tires, for example, might be needed every 3,000 to 4,000 miles and cost about $100 per set. But the good news is that if you're only biking a couple hundred miles, you won't even come close to needing replacements.

On the more extreme end of touring for free, if you learn basic bicycle maintenance, you can take care of most problems on your own. Often, used parts can be found simply having been discarded.

Now, before setting out there are usually upfront costs, but you *can* learn to build your own bike and keep it free. There are numerous "earn a bike" community programs where you volunteer for a certain number of hours at a bike shop and then get to build your own with their parts. You can even make panniers out of crates or buckets.

Food: The cost of food ranges, beginning at the free mark depending on how you ride. I biked 1,000 miles from Madison, Wisconsin to New York City living 100% off food from grocery store dumpsters. In fact, the whole trip was done without a penny in my pocket.

Food is often a main expense, but in countries like the US where we—especially our grocery stores—waste so much perfectly good food, you can travel with literally no money.

Every person's eating style is unique, but most cyclists on a budget will want a camp stove so that wherever they are they can just make themselves a hot meal. It seems that peanut butter sandwiches are pretty essential to a lot of cyclists—you can always find a loaf of bread and peanut butter. Energy bars and the like are prevalent, but I try to eat as much natural, non-packaged food as possible.

Accommodation: There are numerous peer-to-peer options for staying with people for free. Namely, **Warmshowers.org**—a network specifically for hosting cyclists—and **Couchsurfing.com**, WorkAway, HelpX, and WWOOF.

Personally, I rarely pay for a place to sleep since I carry a tent; it's also almost always free to camp in national forests. BLM land, which stands for Bureau of Land Management, consists of millions of acres of free camping, mostly in the western

INSIDER INFO: Warmshowers, Couch-stays, WorkAway, HelpX, and WWOOF? What's Rob talking about? Stay tuned for Part Three!

US. You can camp on BLM land for up to two weeks in the same spot. There's so much land where you can legally pull off on the side of the road, go 100 yards, and just camp for the night. There are plenty of online maps to find the closest spots at **BLM.gov**.

What you'll find is that accommodation while touring is often very different from most people's version of travel, because you cover so many miles in a day, and you often just end up staying wherever works. The goal is to find a good quiet place, like cemeteries, a church, behind a church, public parks, or fire stations. For those last three options, it often helps to ask in advance, and in my experience, firefighters are the best of the bunch. You can even just knock on people's front door and say, "Hey, I'm cycling across the country. I'm looking for a place to set up my tent, could I use your backyard?"

There's a term called "stealth camping" where you're basically ... hiding. That's something that most tour cyclists become accustomed to without planning on it. Say it's getting dark and you haven't reached your destination. You're tired, you need to set up your tent, and you want to go to bed, so you often just find a park, patch of trees, or a river, set up your tent, and take off in the morning for another day of riding.

As you get into paid options, some people travel really light with almost no gear and stay at a hotel every night and eat out for every meal, every day. They'll do things like use CO_2 pumps on their tires, which costs money every time, versus a regular ol' hand pump, which is free. The budget for those costly habits can run you up to $150 a day.

Cycling Cost Summary: My trips really just range. On my second trip across the country I left with $2,000 dollars in cash—no cards and no bank account. By the halfway mark, it was down to about $400. At that point, I gave the rest of the money away and cycled the rest with nothing. So that trip was $1,600. But, roughly summarized, I would say you could comfortably cycle around 3,000 miles as a thrifty traveler for under $2,000 within three months.

EfN: Any thoughts on staying safe?

Whether it's to work or school, on the highway or the interstate, or on the streets, often the most dangerous thing you can do on a common day is ride through fog. Do what you have to do to make sure you're visible. Have a tall, brightly colored flag attached to the bike flying around five feet over your head. Wear a brightly colored safety vest. Group riding definitely helps with safety—more people means more visibility.

Another big rule is not to ride at night. Make a goal of getting up and starting your day early to be done riding before it gets dark. You may also need time to set up camp while it's still light.

Practice bicycle safety just as you would driving safety. It's usually just the law, but it also helps reduce tension between car drivers and cyclists. Do your best to constantly be aware and have your guard up—especially on busy roads. A rearview mirror greatly helps with this, and they're easy to attach to a bike or helmet for under $20.

For women bicyclists, the more planning, the more safety. Know where you'll be at the end of the night, and share your plans with someone you trust. Use the hosting websites I mentioned earlier. Or, consider staying in "official" campgrounds or paid accommodation versus going solo on public land. The key is not to put yourself in isolated, vulnerable situations. If possible, find a travel partner!

EfN: How about the sustainability component?

For people who truly want to reduce their environmental impact, cycle touring is a great method. Living a more environmentally friendly life is almost inherent in the process—you can literally do it without any electronics or waste.

I recommend carrying basic gear that minimizes trash: a reusable water bottle, storage and food containers, reusable bags, etc. Find local farmers' markets and support local business as much as possible. They'll probably want to support you back just out of enthusiasm for your trip!

EfN: How do you recommend choosing a route?

There are so many options that it's best to begin researching areas of interest online. An important thing to remember is that you don't have to start with a giant trip. Just start with a one- or two-day camping trip. Once you've done that, try a week-long tour. Once you've done *that*, do something bigger like biking across a region or a country. Or, just try to bike the farthest you've ever biked in a day. Maybe the farthest you've ever biked is 10 miles, so make a goal of doing 20. Then do two 30-mile days, or a 60-mile total trip.

Those two ideas will help you get the feel of pacing and what gear you prefer. The point is, you can have an amazing cycle tour that is fairly short, and it can still be life-changing.

EfN: Any other hacks, tips, or tools?

Always try to give more than you receive in as many ways as you can. Traveling with a purpose makes the entire experience *so much* better. Here's what I mean by that: most travelers set out with a purpose of simply seeing and exploring their destination. There's nothing wrong with that—personal fulfilment is a great purpose. But when I say "travel with a purpose," I mean go with a desire to make the place you're headed a better place *or* raise awareness about an important issue.

Clean up trash along the route, create a college bike trip to raise awareness about important issues, find sponsorships to raise funds for grassroots or nonprofits. Plus, cycling for an issue makes other people want to get involved, so you end up helping more than just the issue itself. People you meet along the way get excited, so you give them an opportunity to feel good by helping.

What's more, others are so much more likely to host or invite you to their home for a meal or just a hug if you've broken down. They're more likely to give you a ride or bring you to a bike shop. It makes the trip so much more enjoyable when you are not just doing it for yourself.

To spread the word about your trip, you can put a sign on the back of the bicycle or fly a flag that has the cause printed on it. I generally recommend having a blog so that people can feel more involved and follow the adventure. If not a blog, use social media to let people know what you're doing.

Another thing I should mention is that if you're an introvert, be ready to interact with people nearly everywhere you go. They will be asking about where you came from and where you're going. You get the same questions all the time. On the bright side, it's hard to get lonely when you're cycle touring since people are always making conversation and wanting to be involved.

I'd like to give another shout-out to Warmshowers.org, because it can really change everything. It's just an amazing network for cyclers that ends up being more about hospitality than showers. When you're out on the road, hospitality is often what you crave most.

EfN: Would you tell us a tale from the road?

My friend and I are biking cross-country through Nebraska when we look up to see a giant storm approaching with huge dark gray clouds—quite possibly a tornado. It's worrisome—*very*—because we're out in the great plains of Nebraska with nowhere to take cover.

We're cycling on, just staring at the sky and wondering what to do, when this old beat-up 80s truck drives up alongside us. A middle-aged guy, who strikes me as a little bit scary, leans over and shouts through the passenger window, "Do you need a place to take cover from the storm?" All we can say is, "Um ... yes." So he says, "Alright. Look up ahead, you see that row of trees? Just turn in there and that's it."

So then he drives up there, and it's starting to feel like the start of a scary movie. Nonetheless, we all agree it's our best option. We ride up and it turns out to be a little farm. Animals are just everywhere! There are baby cats everywhere and the nicest, fluffiest dog in the world.

A woman comes out of the house and welcomes us, introducing herself as Marsha, the man's wife. In less than a minute, we realize, "Oh, these are just very nice people. We were wrong about *any* other idea."

We end up having a delicious dinner and a wonderful night. The next morning, Marsha sends us off with frozen bags of recently picked cherries from their tree.

That's just one story, but also an example of what's normal. Things like that happen all the time when you're cycle touring. People just want to help you out!

Thanks, Rob!

Who needs credit cards, engines, or even hitch-ready thumbs when there's the ever-dependable, people-powered bicycle? (Okay, thumbs *are* helpful for bicycling, but you get my point.) Up until now, you've probably shunned cycle touring as something only for the ultra-fit, the ultra-crunchy, or some other group apart from yourself. No more excuses, my friend! It's time to hit the road, and there's a well-known saying that comes to mind—perhaps you've heard it: "It's as easy as riding a bike."

The saying is, uh, said for a reason, and if you've dismissed it as just an overused adage, now you know better. But cycle touring is not *just* an easy way to travel for free; it's also a way to live—to come to know yourself in a way that only hours of meditative repetitive motion can teach you and to open yourself up barrier-free to the world around you, and thus the world of travel (and magic!). And it's all as easy as, well, you get the point.

Chapter 10:
I Think You Can, I Think You Can!

While it's unlikely you can use travel hacking or other legal means for *free* bus or train tickets, there are still useful ways to cut the costs. Since my hunch is that you'll hop on one of these transporters at some point during your travels, I still want to share my budget-friendly secrets. We're getting comprehensive up in here!

They may take longer, have more stops, *and* be less comfortable, but let it be said here in black and white: trains and buses are underrated.

If you plan it just right, you can use all that time for stunning window tourism and productive endeavors like reading, journaling, studying, meditating, or making friends with the locals.

Most westerners consider train and bus travel to be a European thing, but stellar routes are alive and well all over the world. Perhaps they're a bit more rickety in smaller regions or third world countries, but they still tend to be a fast, cost-effective, and relatively comfortable way to get around.

When deciding to book between trains and buses, choose not only based on price and time, but also on the views along the route. If all options seem similar, I say choose the choo-choo (train). Whether train or bus, ticket prices typically change over time—usually going up the longer you wait to purchase. Check early for budget fares and sign up online for price notifications when possible. Just pay attention to these alerts and act quickly, because that route may sell out, especially if it's a popular one!

Hop-on, Hop-off or Point-to-Point?

A hop-on, hop-off pass (a.k.a., railpass to some; a HoHo pass to me because fun-to-say words are my jam) allows you to stop (hop off) at various points along a route without committing to a fixed itinerary, then pick up the route (hop on) again whenever you want. Well, *almost* whenever. Usually it covers a specific

> **Ho No!** Some HoHo passes come with tourism offers like lodging or touristy attraction discounts, but using one of these benefits may count as a travel day.

date range with a set of itinerary options, and often there are limits on the number of HoHo rides you can take per day. Just, you know, read the fine print.

When deciding whether a HoHo pass is for you, simply compare its price to the total price of regular, non-HoHo, point-to-point tickets for the itinerary you desire. I won't get into the nitty-gritty because this book is about *free*, but have a look at the article titled "Should I Get a Rail Pass?" on RickSteves.com for more information.

> **MY TAKE:** Because I tend to stay planted somewhere for a couple weeks or more, HoHo passes rarely work for me; they expire before I can take full advantage. Plus, I prefer the variety, freedom, and flavor of taking different types of transportation or lesser-known side routes.

Many countries have HoHo options; websearch "hop-on hop-off route in [country name]" or "bus/rail pass in [country name]." (Pro tip? Don't search "HoHo Pass." You won't get any relevant or mature results.) **Railpass.com** may be the most popular website for European HoHos (author note: my editor actually lol'd at that HoHo), but if you're traveling in Asia, New Zealand, and Australia try **StrayTravel.com**. For Europe, Asia, or Morocco, **Busabout.com** is your online HoHo go-to.

As for point-to-point transportation, try **GoEuro.com** for Europe, **Megabus.com** for North America, and **12go.asia** for Asia (duh!).

Booking the Ride

Once you know your desired destinations, use a travel fare-aggregator or metasearch engine (like **Wanderu.com**, **Rome2Rio.com**, **Loco2.com**, or other region-specific sites) to view route possibilities. This will also allow you to explore price differences and if it makes more sense to book each leg of your trip separately.

Booking rules are different in each country, and delving into them is a whole book unto itself. With buses, your best bet is to websearch "best bus companies in [country name]" or "bus from [country A] to [country B]." With trains, use a fare aggregator to analyze route options, but don't purchase before checking the country's national train website—prices can be cheaper there.

Here is where to begin for a few popular countries when it comes to trains:

Europe: Bahn.de or GoEuro.com	China: china-diy-travel.com/en/ ChinaHighlights.com	Japan: hyperdia.com/en/ or Japan-Rail-Pass.com
⇨ Reservations usually open 90 days in advance. ⇨ Mainly important to book ahead if you want a specific seat/class.	⇨ Reservations usually open 30 days in advance. ⇨ Very important to book ahead.	⇨ Only important to reserve early if traveling during a busy period. ⇨ Prices rarely change no matter when you book, and rail travel is expensive, so a HoHo is worth considering since it provides flexibility without too much of a price difference.

Asia: 12GO.Asia/en	India: ETrain.info or IndiaRailInfo.com	Israel: Rail.co.il/en
⇨ Reservations usually open 60 days in advance. ⇨ Mostly important to book ahead if you want a specific seat or class.	⇨ Reservations usually open 120 days in advance. ⇨ Very important to book ahead.	⇨ No need to book in advance.

Visit **Travelnotes.org** for a broader look at international starting points and **NomadicNotes.com** for Asia-specific information. For overall route information and general advice for several other countries and cities, advice from The Man in Seat 61 at **Seat61.com** is a must.

ACHTUNG! Some websites require that you retrieve the ticket in the country of *purchase* versus the country of *departure*. For example, if you buy a ticket to Spain on Spain's national train website, but you're located in Italy, you may be required to (magically?!) retrieve the ticket from a kiosk *in Spain*. Before purchasing online, ensure you're allowed to print or pick up the ticket in your *departure* country. Otherwise, purchase the ticket at a local station as early as possible.

Boost the odds: Bonus Tips and Reminders

⇨ Nighttime and slower routes are often cheapest.

⇨ When traveling long-distance, overnight rides can kill *three* birds with one stone:

1. No paying for nightly accommodation
2. Fares are often cheaper
3. If you can sleep, time will fly!

⇨ If ticket sales haven't opened and you want to book accommodation at your destination, go for it. But make sure it's with lodgings that won't penalize for date changes or last-minute cancellations. Generally, you can predict the availability of future routes based off current ones.

⇨ Always pack your own meals, snacks, and water (see Chapter 17).

⇨ When retrieving pre-purchased tickets at the station, agents will typically ask to see the same credit card you used to buy the ticket.

⇨ If booking a trip that passes through other travel hubs, check to see if splitting the fare as separate legs makes it cheaper.

⇨ Round-trip fares may be cheaper than one-way, whether or not you use the return ticket.

⇨ Check for student and other age-related member discounts.

⇨ Look for group discounts. This can get tricky when each traveler's name is printed on a single ticket and one of you doesn't show up on departure day. Read the group discount conditions in the fine print.

⇨ Be flexible with dates and examine prices on various days.

⇨ Research the landscape you'll be passing through—put the devices away and take in the outstanding scenery whizzing by outside.

⇨ A stopover along your route can be an added bonus to your itinerary (flexibility!). You can usually store your stuff in a station rental locker. For the cost of some pocket change, you'll get a taste of a location you wouldn't have thought to see otherwise.

You've made it! But where are you staying? The good news is there are plenty of ways to find a free place to hunker down. Choosing what that hunkering looks like depends on your travel style. Maybe you already know what that is, and maybe you're reading this book to figure it out.

If it's that latter option, let's figure this out right now, shall we? Ask yourself what you want in a trip. Is full leisure time your preference? Are you hoping to gain professional experience for a resume? Do you just want to strap on that money wallet and be the ultimate tourist? Is there a cliff-diving spot or hiking trail you refuse to avoid? What else are you after when traveling?

Once you have your travel style figured out, your next step to finding a free place to call temporary home is knowing how long you'll be travelling. For a slower-paced, reflective, or skill-building trip of 10 days or more, a housesit or work-exchange is probably your best bet. If your travel time is limited, but you're a tourism fiend who needs to be on a sightseeing bus or tied to the end of a bungee cord, consider a less demanding housesit, couchstay, or campground, since they don't always require your full presence.

INSIDER INFO: If you're reluctant to ditch resort life, start with a beautifully located housesit or work-exchange that requires only a few hours of "work" time (more on this in later chapters). I've experienced the high life using every method, except going the free route means I don't stuff myself with restaurant food, I get a more authentic experience, and, well, it's *free!*

So, you've got your style, you've got a timeframe, and now we get down to business. To estimate the availability of free accommodation options in your desired destination, research current free options. You don't want to book plane tickets for two months in tropical Phuket, only to discover there are just two hosts available. (Although at the time of writing this book, with just a few keystrokes and mouse clicks, I found 10 Phuket work-exchange hosts between HelpX and Workaway and over 1,000 couchstays available on Couchsurfing.com!)

To start brainstorming your travel schedule, give yourself anywhere from three days to a month to arrange couchstays; hosts don't usually schedule further out than that. The sweet spot for work-exchanges and housesits is usually three to six months in advance—waiting until the last minute and you risk losing the highly sought-after locations. Then again, if you're the gambling type, great opportunities often do pop up only a few days in advance. But, like I said, it's gamble.

In the following chapters, we'll talk more about the free accommodation options, then close things out with an overview of budget choices when free isn't for you. No matter the method you choose, don't forget to kick things off by using that good ol' social network. With six degrees of separation, an offhand comment or online post might lead you to staying with someone else's friends or family. Post a picture of your destination on Instagram or give the scoop on Facebook, including something like, "Can't wait to land in Russia … have you been? Where should I stay? What should I do!?" Never hurts to see who'll step up!

 ## Interlude: Toilets, Fleas, and Family / Nazareth, Israel

"Are you aiming for the seat or are you aiming for the water?"

In unsteady Spanish, I've finally worked up the courage to ask Marcos the burning question I've harbored since my first morning at Eitan and Sofía's house. Why am I speaking Spanish? Why is this man staying at my host's home? And why is he peeing *all over* the toilet seat each night?

Many such questions have formed since my arrival here. There's the Marcos/pee issue, but there is also this: Why, exactly, do my hosts want volunteers in the first place?

Let's backtrack a bit to my setup in Israel's southernmost town of Eilat, where Mr. Jams and I have been living. You might recall, our apartment is a cramped, perma-hot, 200-square-foot room in which I spend most of my time avoiding the even hotter outdoors. Mr. Jams works from sun up to sun down, and I go a little crazy with the solitude. Things have become stifling (again) since my return from the "zoo" and I feel the need to escape (again).

Scanning online for work-exchange hosts in Israel, the relaxed and creative vibe of Sofía and Eitan's profile stands out. They've spent the past decade making ends meet primarily by building interactive musical playgrounds at schools. Additional income comes from selling handmade arts and crafts at local markets and out of their home-adjacent studio. I send a feeler message to ask about their availability, and Eitan responds asking me to call.

Throwing on my laptop headphones, I dial Eitan and listen to the familiar bubbly Skype call tone. The raspy voice that answers can only be described as an Israeli-equivalent of a California surfer dude. Small talk: Why am I in Israel? Do I like it? Where else have we lived?

Then I ask why they want volunteers. Eitan explains that they need help organizing craft materials, feeding animals, and—most importantly—expanding and tending to their organic garden. He even says the magic phrase: hardly any weeding.

The minimal timing requirements—only two to three hours per day—and prospects of gardening are irresistible, so we agree to a week-long stay. Hanging up, I can already feel the cool air of the north as I book my six-hour bus ride up to Nazareth.

On the way up, I stop in Jerusalem to spend a night with Ella, the fellow volunteer I befriended at the zoo, and her family. Exploring the Jerusalem Farmers Market, we reminisce about our week at the zoo and the narrowly avoided volunteer exploitation it entailed (another story for another time). We end the night with Ella's mother's swoonworthy home-cooked meal of borscht and crusty bread while listening to the drone of Russian news coming from the living room.

Then, onward to another Holy Land. The dusty bus rolls to a stop and I spot a smiling man with shaggy brown hair, tanned skin, a tank top, and board shorts. No doubt it's Eitan. He's small but wiry, and easily throws my bag into the back of his old pickup truck. We take off through a barren landscape of tilled fields and treeless knolls. The area, he explains, is named *Megiddo*, which roughly translates to "Armageddon." Things are looking up.

His home comes into view as we drive up the dirt driveway, and I scan excitedly for signs of the garden. He points to a plot of dirt the size of a Ford pickup. "That's it," says Eitan pointing to the dirt. "We haven't started yet. Maybe in a few weeks."

I suppress annoyance—gardening experience was the main reason for choosing this exchange—but chalk the misunderstanding up to Eitan's forgivable personality. I've already begun to better understand it—he's the "artistic" type and, I suspect, a fellow ADD (attention *different*) person. He also smokes bountiful quantities of weed—something ill-known for improving attention span.

When we spoke on the phone weeks earlier, he probably *intended* to have a garden by now. But that desire was probably forgotten within seconds of hanging up.

He shifts the truck into park and I take in my surroundings: slightly dilapidated two-story home, a front porch cluttered with rocking chairs and unused children's toys, three scraggly cats, and a litter of dusty kittens. There's a small dirt arena with a listless donkey and a miniature horse. Two big, lazy, and probably very old dogs lounge on the cement porch of a wall-less art studio. It's no paradise, but I'm not here to sip mai tais and work on my tan, so I focus on the positive: Eitan is fun and relaxed, there are kittens, there's an art studio, and I'm not in Eilat.

We pick our way through the front porch and find the whole family waiting in the kitchen. Sofía smiles big with their year-old son in her arms and greets me with a hug in her native Argentinian patois. Four-year-old Alicia performs various tumbles on the living room floor, and two beautiful teenage girls from Sofía's previous marriage stand at the edge of the room and smile like the disinterested teens they are.

Something big is coming down the stairs. Enter Marcos. He and Eitan became friends a decade ago when living in Marcos's native country of Chile. Currently down on his luck, he's staying with the family for a few months.

Sofía leads me upstairs to my room where I deposit my bags. It neighbors Marcos's bedroom, and the rest of the family sleeps on the ground floor. With four work-exchanges under my belt, I expect Sofía, like previous hosts, to begin showing me the projects I'll be working on. Instead, she tells me to relax and get settled, then returns downstairs without further instruction.

Instead of relax and get settled, I do the opposite: I fret over the unknown. Instead of spending this time getting to know them or simply sitting down with them to watch TV, I shut myself in my room, unpack, and begin anxiously surfing the web. I'm already considering an escape.

The next morning, I choose muesli amidst a few cereal options and have a lazy breakfast alone. Sofía watches TV with the two youngest, and there are no signs of human life anywhere else. I still don't know what I'll be

work-exchanging on and feel anxious about my inactivity.
I build the courage to ask Sofía to put me to work, but
she just tosses her dreadlocks behind her shoulder and
laughs a bit. "It's fine," she reassures me. "Just relax.
Maybe ask Eitan."

Because they've already fed me two meals and given me
a place to sleep, I'm overtaken by a need to feel productive. I catch Eitan a couple hours later before he
heads off somewhere with Marcos. He pauses, pensive, and
suggests we walk over to the art studio.

About the size of an elementary school classroom, the
studio overflows with intricate and colorful projects.
Workstations are spaced throughout the room: one with glue
guns and pieces for jewelry; another with string, hooks,
and stones or polished charms; and another with fabrics,
markers, pencils, and a variety of drawing surfaces.

It's an artist's paradise and a child's heaven. After
30 minutes' worth of show-and-tell, I'm still unsure of
what he actually wants me to *do*, so I ask.

"Well, you can do what you like. If you find something
interesting … maybe you can make some earrings? Or keychains? The kids like keychains, and you can put anything
you like on them—a rock, a feather. Maybe if you see something that needs organizing, you can. Whatever you like."

This isn't work. It's summer camp! I'm being given the
gift of *complete creative freedom*, yet I'm frozen by the
fear of failing. I want specifics. I want parameters. What
if the feather keychain I make for some child is *wrong*?

Eitan leaves me in the studio, and I sit on a tree
trunk-cum-bench to begin an emotionally uncomfortable and
very tentative arts and crafts session. Rifling through
small drawers of wires, beads, and rocks with holes drilled
through them, I lay out my materials. I stare. I stand
up. First, I should inspect the completed keychains. You
know, to ensure I follow the right style.

Sitting back down, I toy with possible bauble and
feather arrangements as the dogs lazily sulk in and out,
leaving their furry flyaways everywhere for me to brush
away. But then a bead rolls off the table and as I lean
down to pick it up, I see them.

The fleas. My legs are covered! *Abort mission*!

Frantically slap-wiping myself down, beads and feathers
scatter as I abandon my keychain project and flee (so to
speak) the studio, kicking up desert dust like a camel as
I search for Sofía.

Panic begins taking over as I process what this means for me. If they only want assistance in the studio, I'm doomed! This work-exchange will be all for naught. I *can't* go back in there. Ever.

I find Sofía on the living room floor with the kids watching a Spanish soap opera while twirling a dreadlock in her fingers. Trying to calm my breathing, I search my Spanish.

"Hi … Sofía … there are a lot of fleas in the studio …"

"Ohhh, right," she nods. "Yes, it's the dogs. We're having a tough time keeping them out."

Nodding in return, I try to parse my next words judiciously, but instead I blurt, "I just counted 18 on my legs and I don't think I can work in there."

"Okay, that's fine," she replies as if it's not the first time she's hearing this. "You can just relax and we'll figure something out when Eitan gets back."

That could take all day. "Is there anything else you would like me to do?"

"Oh, no, just *relaaax*."

Me being me, I do anything but. Sequestering myself in my room has become my go-to when I hear the word "relax," so I ascend the stairs, my inner monologue on autopilot: *Do they want me to work? Are they just looking for company? Do they feel like I am cheating them? HOW CAN I PROVE MYSELF?!*

The week passes with me jumping at any chance to pitch in and prove I'm helpful. One day, Eitan shows up with a truckload of discarded grocery store arugula—hundreds of bunches bound by tiny blue rubber bands. We spend hours removing them before feeding the greens to the horse and donkey.

Another work session keeps me outside sanding wood pieces for five hours with an old tooth-polishing apparatus. The next day, I convince Sofía to let me organize the overflowing kitchen cabinets, and in this productive state I find myself comfortably connecting with her.

If I'm worried about seeming like an ungrateful guest, Marcos certainly isn't. He lounges like a pro and sneaks away on mysterious field trips with Eitan during the day. Sometimes at night, long after we've all gone to bed, he gets up to pee and almost always manages to leave some on the toilet seat. When I finally confront him after enduring five days of this, he miraculously manages to kick the habit.

Toward the end of my stay, Eitan invites me to his parents' Shabbat dinner. Shabbat, the Jewish Sabbath, begins on Friday evening with a sumptuous traditional dinner, blessings, upbeat songs, and familial connection. It's similar to the Christian Sunday, which is often spent resting and in worship, but the Jewish Sabbath concludes on Saturday evening at sunset.

We all pile into Eitan's truck and hit the road to his parents' bustling home. Eitan's mom tends a stovetop with every burner occupied. There are boiled potatoes, fried chicken cutlets, hearty beef stew, and chicken and vegetable soup. I peek in the oven to see a steaming dish of apricot chicken.

Three teenage granddaughters giggle together in the living room and yarmulke-wearing grandsons tease them or wrestle with each other. Eitan catches up with his brother and sister-in-law, who live a very different lifestyle as ultra-religious Hasidic Jews. We all talk and rest, and in a house where I'm not work-exchanging, I take leave of my self-induced anxiety.

After the candles are lit to usher in the Sabbath, we sit at the table adorned with a maze of covered pots and fresh salads. A bulging loaf of challah is covered but beckons to be broken, while small bowls of pickles, olives, tzatziki, and matzo crackers fill in the empty spaces on the table. Mild white wine and grape juice are poured as the men scramble to find their yarmulkes before Eitan's father blesses a cup of wine and the covered challah.

Growing up without religion, I have never experienced anything like this. It's culturally overwhelming … and I love it.

When dinner winds to a close, Eitan's father collapses onto the couch and I sit in a nearby armchair. The record player lies between us, and when I begin scanning through his albums, a treasure trove is revealed: Simon and Garfunkel, The Temptations, Paul Anka! I bond with the patriarch over his spectacular vinyl collection as he recounts his love of American music acquired in his youth during the '60s.

Lying back on the chair, watching this family mingle and enjoy each other's company, I think regretfully about the way I've spent the past week obsessing over showing my value through work. Like divine intervention, it finally clicks: I am not here to prove myself useful to anyone. I am here to be me.

⚡ Chapter 11:
Work-Exchange

Traveling for more than two weeks and don't want to spend a dime? *Helloooo*, work-exchange! It's a wildly underrated free travel method that lets you travel indefinitely. Room and board are completely free, you learn new skills, get your hands a little dirty (literally and metaphorically), and actually *live* in a place instead of just seeing it through the tourist looking glass.

Going somewhere sunny to lounge by a pool, sip fancy cocktails, and eat indulgent dinners day after day can get boring. Work-exchange is your cure for boring because it's one of the best ways to jump into the new and unfamiliar. You could be milking goats in the hills of the French Pyrenees, caring for kids as an *au pair* in India, or running a hostel in Thailand.

It takes a special kind of courage to decide that your next trip will involve meeting new people, getting along with those people, and sharpening skills with them on a daily basis. Unlike the short burst of adrenaline you get with a quick Machu Picchu excursion, work-exchanges are sustained, immersive, and *true* life adventures that simply can't be had as a casual tourist.

What Is Work-Exchange and Is It for You?

In a nutshell, work-exchange is an online community made up of autonomous hosts and workers (aka "volunteers") who each create profiles detailing what they're looking for in an exchange. There are no hard-and-fast rules to how it works, but the general standard is that volunteers work anywhere from 20 to 30 hours over three to five days per week. In return, hosts provide three square meals per day, culture, camaraderie, and a cozy place to sleep.

Check out this work-exchange math:

If we factor a weekly average of 25 volunteer hours and 56 sleep hours (eight per night), that leaves 87 waking hours to do as you please:

7 days x 24 hours = 168 hours per week
– 25 hours of work
– 56 hours of sleep
= 87 hours of playtime!

I'll clarify: if you take a work-exchange trip with these hours, more than *half* of your time could be used for pure and profligate fun … in another country … with free food and accommodation!

Of course, the schedule above is fairly simple (do we always get eight hours of sleep every night?). Some hosts might require six hours of work per day for six days a week, while others might ask for only three hours for three days. Sometimes you'll work and eat with the host and other volunteers, and sometimes you'll be alone. Hosts may ask that you follow a fixed schedule, or they may simply tell you what needs to be done and leave you to do it. Whatever your host prefers, as their volunteer, you're expected to follow their lead.

Every host home is different—sometimes *very* different. So, prepare yourself: you'll be completely immersed in the lives of strangers. But they won't be strangers for long! The circumstances are often surprising and unpredictable, but these interpersonal experiences can provide some of the most transformative and enhancing times of your life.

If you're not yet sold on work-exchange, here are **nine more ways** to tell if it's something to explore:

1. Affordability is a priority.

Once you get to a host's home, you don't have to spend a dime. If you use free transport, you can "job hop" to other work-exchanges and live the nomadic life indefinitely. You won't necessarily *make* money, but you won't lose it, either.

2. You're looking for a long-term experience.

There are endless amounts of work-exchange opportunities. If you don't want to job hop too much, you can hunker down in one or two of them for months (even years!) at a time.

3. You want to deal with "real" people.

Work-exchange usually takes place at a person's home, not in a professional workplace. This means you're interacting with owners, decision-makers, and mommies, not administrators, middle-managers, and memos. In other words, these exchanges may seem less organized, but if you're self-starting and enjoy autonomy, go for it!

Less red tape and fewer hierarchies also mean that there are no higher-ups to report to if there are problems. An email can be sent to work-exchange program coordinators, but ultimately it's you who's responsible for any undertaken risk or conflict.

4. You're feeling lost or unfocused.

There is nothing wrong with being aimless and wanting to explore various options. I won't get too zen-on-the-mountain here, but the truth is that every step you take is a step in the direction that's right *for you*. The important thing is to just take steps—you won't learn anything about yourself if you don't try anything new.

Before I set out on the work-exchange odyssey of my early 20s, I knew I loved working with food, but I had no idea where to start. My international business degree didn't exactly train me in this realm. I also knew I didn't want to detract from that love by poring over graduate school applications, toiling in the job hunt trenches, or going through weeks of job training. Work-exchange was my perfect solution—it gave me the chance to work in various food-related fields, then move on whenever I wanted!

5. You want to learn new skills or gain work experience.

As mentioned, when I began work-exchanging it was partly to broaden my food education. Whether it was through eating, living with amazing cooks, helping in restaurants, animal husbandry, or growing and foraging, I quickly grew my food resume. I skipped the usual requisite schooling and uncomfortable job interviews while acquiring skills that would've taken years if I had gone the traditional route.

But work-exchanges offer way more than just food experiences. Check out this list of **things I've dabbled in** (and you can, too!):

- ⇨ Wool shearing and looming
- ⇨ Goat and sheep herding
- ⇨ Goat milking
- ⇨ Cheese, ricotta, and yogurt-making
- ⇨ Event planning and catering
- ⇨ Zookeeping (being chased by a camel, courted by an ostrich, and cuddled by a coati)
- ⇨ Chicken-coop building
- ⇨ Cement laying
- ⇨ Wood chopping and stacking (stacking is an art!)
- ⇨ Hemp and limestone construction
- ⇨ Wet and dry stone walling
- ⇨ Social media promotion & blogging

⇨ Bed and breakfast maintenance

⇨ Jewelry making

⇨ Large-scale farming (ever planted 3,000 artichokes?)

⇨ Animal slaughter: poultry, swine, and rabbit (full disclosure: I only watched.)

⇨ Orchard maintenance & pruning

⇨ Wild food foraging

⇨ Running a British pub

⇨ Professional baking & cookery

⇨ Landscape architecture

⇨ Guided tours (through the Tuscan countryside, no less)

⇨ Garden creation

⇨ Limestone construction

⇨ Eco-tourism management

⇨ Composting (kitchen, garden, and toilet)

⇨ Vegetable gardening

⇨ Food preservation

⇨ Traditional French, Israeli, Turkish, Greek, German, Swiss, Spanish, Irish, British, and Italian cookery

6. You're unemployed or retired.

Trouble finding a job? Taking a sabbatical? Work-exchange should be high priority. Here's why: you can gain actual field experience and useful highlights on your resume. Most employers *like* seeing that you've ventured outside the norm and broadened your horizons with travel. (Hint: you don't have to mention it's because you were unemployed!)

Also, retirement doesn't have to mean the end of work for you. You can make up for the time you lost in the rat race, or you can use a work-exchange to feed your adventurous side. You might even find yourself mentoring some of your younger work-exchange co-volunteers.

7. You have specialized or specific skills.

If you have specialized training (e.g., carpentry, social media, electrical work, computer programming), you may already have a winning piece of the work-exchange pie. Your advantage is a simple result of supply and demand. Hosts might welcome the savings that come from paying in room and board rather than the expenses of a costly contractor. You might even be able to negotiate fewer work hours in exchange for your expertise. This can be a delicate negotiation—consider how to approach each host carefully and remember it's all about symbiosis.

8. You simply want a new living situation.

Work-exchange is a great way to live somewhere rent-free and, like I said, do whatever you want in your free time. You can run a business remotely or finish that book you've been writing. You don't even have to go abroad—there's a good chance that you can find somewhere in the next town over!

9. You want to learn about other cultures or languages.

It's obvious, but there's no better way to get to know a place than by living with locals. Moreover, you'd be hard-pressed to find a quicker method to learn a foreign language than with complete immersion!

"Wait! Is it really okay to travel before starting my career?"

Here's the deal, Sporto:

There's a very simple reason why leadership roles in companies are so out of reach for newbies: no experience. Some people might bypass this disadvantage with a postgraduate degree, but the truth is that even if you *have* the time and money for grad school, it may not be worth it.

Solution? The *school of life*, where anyone can go.

The school of life will teach you plenty: leadership skills, relationship management, business administration, international relations, wool shearing (okay, perhaps not *directly* relevant). You name it, and you can probably find it in this school's course syllabus.

Additionally, the more life experience we have, the more capable we are of problem-solving, handling surprises and stress, multitasking, and communicating. What company *wouldn't* want an employee with those skills? Whether blue- or white-collar, entrepreneur or not, field experience is a sure-fire path to being invaluable to most businesses.

In short: traveling will *not* delay your career goal-setting. It will move you forward with an unforgettable and unique edge over your peers.

Feeling better, Sporto?

Getting Started

Before I list the best places to start looking for work-exchanges, you should know that the best ones charge for memberships. **HelpX.net** and Workaway.info each charge about $30 for a two-year membership and both provide access to hosts all over the world, without limitation. WWOOF, on the other hand, usually charges anywhere from $30 to $70 per year, on a *per-country* basis. Based on this, I'll let you decide which sites are worth your time and money.

On HelpX and Workaway, you can peruse all work-exchange offerings before registering; Workaway even lets you read other volunteer reviews before registering. Start with keyword searches to find appealing options based on your interests, such as construction, cooking, and children; or you might base it on hobbies like yoga, sailing, or woodworking. The world is your oyster! Keep searching until something piques your interest, and take your time since this is also a way to familiarize yourself with the system.

As you peruse these profiles, consider what it is you're truly seeking. Is it work experience? Cultural exchange? Interpersonal connections? Host profiles and volunteer reviews should give plenty of clues for what you can expect. Will you have a roommate or living quarters to yourself? How about food—do you have any dietary restrictions? Is the home in a noisy urban area or in a quiet rural town? Would their pet cats make you sneeze? Does the host seem like a grouch? This is the OkCupid-meets-Facebook of work-exchanges. Use it wisely.

The Profile

Once you've decided which site speaks best to your travel goals (I opted for a profile on both HelpX and Workaway), go ahead and register, then create a standout profile. Hosts take a big leap of faith accepting strangers into their homes, so don't skimp on details about your personality. Sell yourself, but be honest! It's for everyone's best interest.

Here's what to include:

⇨ Your home country
⇨ Hobbies and interests
⇨ Education and training
⇨ Professional and/or volunteer experiences
⇨ Foreign language capabilities
⇨ Why you're interested in work-exchange

Feel free to model yours after this sample profile or just use it as inspiration:

Work-Exchange Sample Profile

Hello! I recently left my four-year home in San Francisco to explore the world. I graduated with a degree in Marketing from the University of Vermont, and after that moved to California where I had a few jobs doing social media marketing and restaurant work.

What I really love is working with food and being outdoors, so I'm looking for work-exchange experiences to explore those avenues. This period of travel is something I would like to consider as continued education, so if you feel like I could learn from your work-exchange, we might be a great fit!

I love to cook and garden, and I hope to learn more about growing and harvesting food. I am also very interested in acquiring skills like carpentry, building, and other useful things that you can't really learn in an office.

Some of my skills:

⇨ Advanced Spanish speaker

⇨ Leadership

⇨ Self-starter

⇨ Able to work autonomously

⇨ Able to cook for groups

⇨ Social media development

⇨ Animal care (dogs, cats, goats)

⇨ Experience with group instruction/training

⇨ Fast learner

Skills that I've gained with other work-exchanges include:

⇨ Cheesemaking

⇨ Wood chopping/stacking

⇨ Olive picking

I eat most types of foods and love a nice array of fruits and vegetables when in season. My love of the ocean also tends to steer me away from eating endangered fish species.

Otherwise, I'm pretty laid-back and I don't usually have difficulty sharing space with others. I'm a non-smoker and I try to clean up after myself and do my part for household chores. In my free time I enjoy reading, board games, hiking, and movies.

If this sounds good to you, maybe we'll meet sometime. Thanks for reading!

Finding Your Match

Work-exchanges can be arranged anywhere from a day to over a year in advance. If you know when you want to travel, even if it's approximate timing, start your search. Highly reviewed and sought-after host sites fill up early and often, so contacting them six months to a year in advance gives better odds of scoring that coveted spot. That being said, one of my favorite experiences was with two first-time hosts that I found and booked just one day in advance (Hi, Mick and Lisa!).

If it's your first time, work-exchanging with co-volunteers might be ideal and less lonely, but it depends on your social appetite and how you feel about living with complete strangers. An introvert may not enjoy jumping in with a bunch of new faces. An extrovert, on the other hand, could thrive in that situation.

Some hosts have dozens of glowing reviews, so booking with them is usually a great introduction to the work-ex-change experience. You may also find some hosts with no reviews at all. That's not always a bad thing! It may mean they're new to work-ex-change or that they live in an area that doesn't attract many volunteers. Maybe they've hosted, but used a different platform to find volunteers without a review option. If in doubt, ask if they've hosted

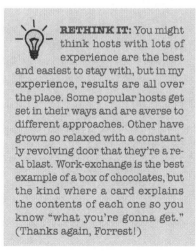

RETHINK IT: You might think hosts with lots of experience are the best and easiest to stay with, but in my experience, results are all over the place. Some popular hosts get set in their ways and are averse to different approaches. Other have grown so relaxed with a constant-ly revolving door that they're a re-al blast. Work-exchange is the best example of a box of chocolates, but the kind where a card explains the contents of each one so you know "what you're gonna get." (Thanks again, Forrest!)

before. If they have, but garnered no reviews, this could be cause to raise an eyebrow.

It's important to get a strong feel for the personalities of hosts before committing to their work-exchange. This is just like online dating: if there's chemistry during your email exchange or phone calls, it could be the perfect match. Why fight the magic?

Making Contact

As you find appealing work-exchange jobs and hosts, remember my dating analogy and begin sending out "feeler messages." These messages help answer three crucial questions:

1. Does the host have space anytime during or around your desired dates?

2. What can you expect to be working on (if it's not covered in their profile)?

3. Do you want to keep corresponding with this host in the hopes it will bring you closer to a decision?

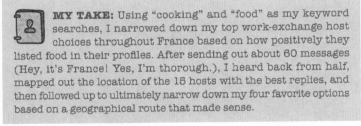

MY TAKE: Using "cooking" and "food" as my keyword searches, I narrowed down my top work-exchange host choices throughout France based on how positively they listed food in their profiles. After sending out about 60 messages (Hey, it's France! Yes, I'm thorough.), I heard back from half, mapped out the location of the 15 hosts with the best replies, and then followed up to ultimately narrow down my four favorite options based on a geographical route that made sense.

It's not always apparent who will respond in time and with desirable answers, so play the odds and send out as many feeler messages as possible to prospective hosts.

The most important goal of the feeler message is to make a great first impression and establish rapport. Hosts may get tons of applications every week. The message is your first impression, so make it count. Show them why they should, ahem, "swipe right" on *you*.

Unless you know exact travel dates and locations, you don't need to commit to any timing in your feeler message; it's okay to say you're still working on an itinerary at this stage. This way, as hosts respond, you can see your options more clearly and then easily decide where you'd like to stay.

PRO TIP: Once a host responds positively, pin their location on a map. I use Google Maps and a color-coded priority system based on which locations sound best. Mapping them out enables you to visualize a travel route that makes sense given your most enticing available options.

Check out the work-exchange feeler message sample below. (Not to be used for online dating.)

Sample Feeler Message:

Bonjour!

My name is Gina Brown and I would love to come visit your slice of beautiful Southern France! Cheese-making is something that has always interested me, so hopefully I can learn about it through your expertise. I'm a hard-worker, and while I don't have hands-on experience with sheep or cheese-making, I'm a quick learner and bet I'd soon be helpful!

As for a little bit about myself, I studied business and have worked mainly in an office as a data analyst, but now I want to explore other professions and lifestyles, which is one of the main reasons I'm traveling. I love cooking, reading, jogging, card games, and new experiences.

I speak only a basic level of French (which I plan on improving during my stay), so hopefully that will not be a problem. Overall I'm a pretty easy-going person and I feel like we might be a great fit.

As for logistics, I'd love to visit sometime during May, June, or July for two to four weeks. My schedule is still flexible because I'm trying to coordinate with a handful of other hosts, so if there are some times that work best for you, please let me know and I'll try to work things out accordingly.

You touch on this in your profile, but given the season I'm looking at, are you able to tell me some specific tasks I can expect to be working on? Also, I'd love to know the work schedule you prefer from volunteers [author's note:*only bring this up if it is not mentioned in the profile*].

If any of this sounds good, please get back to me at your earliest convenience and we can discuss more :)

Merci beaucoup!

Gina

Ironing Out the Details

Now you can lean back while the responses trickle in. As with any written communication, response times will vary. Some respond that day, some take over a week. Thank the dud responders for their time and move on; but with the ones that caught your eye, don't leave them hanging. Thank them as well and let them know you'll be in touch as soon as you are in the later stages of finalizing your travel plans.

When you do actually get to those later stages, your next correspondence with your short-list of hosts should involve ironing out dates and the **finer details of the work-exchange** that haven't been covered up until now, such as:

➯ Work schedules (hours/day, days/week, tasks, duties, etc.)
➯ Dietary restrictions, if any
➯ Living situation (room-mates, rooms, beds, etc.)

I don't believe it's unreasonable to ask for details regarding your basic necessities—food, shelter, work arrangements—but keep these questions to a minimum. Ask what you feel is necessary and remember that part of this whole experience is acceptance of new and unpredictable circumstances. If you have any misgivings, hopping on the phone might be the best option for clarity.

 MY TAKE: I'm a recovering perfectionist; I used to try to "make sure" I got the *best* host in every region. I finally realized that controlling outcomes like that is nearly impossible. Some hosts I envisioned as being stellar were quite the opposite. And some I was leery about were pretty fantastic. Toward the end of my travels, once a host accepted the date I offered and their setup seemed good enough, I muffled my inner FOMO and committed to their offering without looking back.

As some hosts respond, you may be inclined to wait and see who *else* responds before confirming stays with any who *have* responded. FOMO at its finest. My advice? Make plans sooner rather than later and trust that everything will work out—otherwise, you could lose a great opportunity while you wait. Giving hosts five to ten days to respond isn't unreasonable, neither is sending a follow up to the non-responders if you're *really* interested in their offering.

Finally, once correspondence has led you to hammer down the stays you desire, confirm everything with the host and begin making travel arrangements (see Chapter 4)!

 INSIDER INFO: The work-exchange concept isn't quite global yet. So, to someone unfamiliar with it—like a vigilant immigration official—"work-exchange" might sound like you're entering their country to work or volunteer illegally. I'm not offering you legal advice here—if you're concerned, I suggest looking into the country's laws.

That being said, my typical MO is to tell officials that I'm a tourist staying with friends or at a hotel where I've yet to make the reservation (you don't want them to call the hotel and find that you've been, um, kidding). The address I provide *isn't my host's*. Why not? If the host has had many foreign volunteers in the past, their information might get flagged in the system. I know an American who arrived in Ireland and was turned away before leaving the airport, because her host had been flagged for suspicious activity—a direct result of all the foreigners who had used the host's address upon entering the country!

What to Do Upon Arrival

Remember actual blind dates? (Look them up if not. *Sigh.*) When two people agreed, usually reluctantly, to go on a "blind date," neither party knew much about the other beyond what their respective matchmakers (moms, BFFs, frenemies) had described. Showing up to a host's home is similar—you know you've both agreed to this, but you have little idea what to *actually* expect. It could be the last date you ever go on … or just another one to add to your list of "nexts!" Keep an open mind from minute one—it may be the best first minute of the rest of your trip (life!?).

A [Real Live!] Host's Take:

EfN: On a scale of "nervous to excited," how do you feel in those moments before the volunteer shows up?

Mr. Charlie: "Yes. All of the above. Usually we have a good feel for the individual because of our correspondence, but this doesn't always reveal idiosyncrasies (like soup slurping). Sometimes, for whatever reason, we have taken volunteers we weren't entirely sure about or we don't know anything about. Those spur-of-the-moment, last-minute volunteers who show up after a single, brief telephone call can make for awkward moments.

Having said that, we are into our sixth or seventh year of volunteers now, so it has become less of a stress, as the new people couldn't possibly be as bad as some of those who have come and gone. Everything considered, how bad could it be?"

Your host's welcome upon arrival will vary. They may pull out all the stops to make you feel like royalty. Or it may be a quick one because they're busy with work, family, or countless other daily chores. Some are so accustomed to work-exchange volunteers that a new face is as routine as yesterday's dinner. In the words of that super-inspiring Zen master you saw at a TED talk last year, just *go with the flow*.

You might have to keep yourself occupied until the host is done with their day's work. Don't throw your feet up on the table just yet, but *do* relax and try to get settled before your first work day. They might even ask if you could lend a hand with some chores. Arrive without too many expectations and you won't be surprised or disappointed by whatever happens. It's all part of the adventure!

One thing that is 100% within your control is making a great first impression. Bring a little gift like a bar of chocolate or souvenir from home. You're not exactly a guest, but you're also not a new hire trying to impress a boss. Yes, you're playing by the house rules, but it's still a symbiotic exchange. Consider yourself a new colleague in training and follow their lead.

Sooner or later you'll get a chance to talk to your host. Play the *getting to know you* game, but also revisit key topics about work, food, and other day-to-day details. You don't want to deal with an awkward exchange if beef lasagna is on the menu but in your email exchange you said you're a vegetarian. Or maybe they forgot about your

TALES FROM THE ROAD: I tended to go for work-exchanges requiring around 20 weekly work hours. Hey, I like my me time. Of course, there was that one work-exchange on a large farm on Turkey's northern coast. Despite its 36-hour work weeks, it was one of my favorites because it had the best home-cooked food I've ever had . . . ever! Not just in my travels, in my *life*. I worked those hours just to get that food into my belly. It was beyond worth it!

agreed-upon four-hour workdays because the last volunteer did five. Discussing and managing expectations before starting your work-exchange helps to avoid confusion and miscommunication.

Topics to consider revisiting:

➪ Daily work hours, including meals and days off

➪ Host's preferred work style (to-do lists versus one task at a time)

➪ Who you'll be working with, if anyone

Work It!

The "work" portion of your work-exchange usually begins the day after arrival, unless hosts are taking time off (lucky you). Stick to the hours agreed upon, and keep an hourly work log in a place accessible to your host. There's a good chance the host isn't keeping track, so this way you'll do justice to the agreement. Arguably, you should resist the temptation to work *more* than the discussed hours (unless you really, *really* want to!). Here's why:

The Law of Misguided Expectations: If you work extra hours, hosts might come to expect it. It's like being annoyed when chips and salsa aren't free at a Mexican restaurant (at least that's the case with us *Americanos locos*). Doing what's agreed-upon—not much more and definitely not less—prevents confusion, manages their expectations, and allows you to enjoy your free time without hosts feeling left in the dust.

Case in point? I was one of ten volunteers at a farm in France when I had my first run-in with volunteer "exploitation." A couple well-meaning volunteers decided to work eight-hour days alongside the host, and the strange effect was that many of the others (especially newcomers) felt pressured to do the same. Unfortunately, the host kept silent and did nothing to prevent this; his wife even told us that it made him "sad" when some of us stopped working and he had to keep going.

Hosts should not allow this to happen, but preparation will help you escape a tight spot. It's another good reason to discuss expectations before, in correspondence, *and* upon arrival. Nevertheless, exploitative work-exchange hosts are few and far between. Once you settle into the experience, you'll realize just how special it is to experience "home" from a completely different perspective.

Before you get too puffed up as a justice-championing volunteer, remember this: you aren't the only one at risk of exploitation. Even we innocent travelers can get a little too comfortable and take advantage of an unwatchful eye or an overly-accommodating host.

A [Real Live!] Host's Take:

EfN: How do you handle problematic personalities?

Mr. Charlie: The short answer is we ... feed them to the pigs. It is referred to as "makin' bacon."

Okay, the truth of the matter is that *I* have probably more of a problematic personality than anyone who comes to stay, so the onus is on me to try and make it work. This can be trying. Very. Very. Trying.

Here's some obvious advice: be a good worker! While your overarching reason for being there may indeed be your Kerouac-ian desire for a travel experience, during that relatively small amount of time you spend working, make it count. A host I worked for in Greece put it best:

"The worst crime you can commit here is to not care. This is especially true of those volunteers who are travelers first, and volunteers a poor second. We try to weed out people who are obviously looking for a cheap method of travel, rather than a farming experience that happens to be somewhere foreign. The reason is that they don't particularly want to work, and they don't have any enthusiasm for the kind of work they're doing."

The Rhythm of Work-Exchange

As the days go by, you'll settle into a work-exchange rhythm. You might find that there is room to amend your work schedule or request some other adjustments. If it's reasonable to request a different start time, a midday break, or some alone time during meals, do so with respect and without expectation or entitlement.

You might also want to "disappear" when not working. That's fine! There's no pressure to hang out with hosts or co-volunteers during your free time. But be polite—let them know when you plan on missing meals or being unavailable. Sometimes it doesn't hurt to reassure them that you're not displeased or unhappy; find a light-hearted excuse like you're addicted to a good book (an awesome page-turner called *Everywhere for Nothing*, perhaps ...).

MY TAKE: As an introvert, I like more alone time than many. This can be tough when living, working, and sharing meals with the same people every day. If others seem confused by my isolationist tendencies, I'll find a casual way to mention my need for alone time.

My favorite escape is to make and eat breakfast or lunch alone (unless the cook is planning something special). Don't treat their kitchen like an all-you-can-eat buffet. Politely ask for ingredients and other items so you can prepare something for yourself in advance, or go buy a meal elsewhere.

Work-exchange is truly a *lifestyle*. Take the time to connect with and understand your hosts—this may be the greatest reward of all. And if you feel the pull to become a work-exchange nomad, plan your next destination while on the road instead of far in advance. It adds to the spontaneity and keeps you open to travel magic!

Now that you know about work-exchange, go discover some hosts!

 ## Interlude: Luxury by the Sea / Lakonia, Greece

Tensions are high. Mr. Jams is calling out Janet, our host, telling her she's making it all up. She sits placidly poised, impish despite her 72 years. I'm not confident enough to chime in; it seems best to accept my losing fate with a veneer of quiet dignity.

"Is that a challenge?" Janet grins, leaning back in her chair.

Her husband, Wade, is paying staunch attention to something invisible on the far wall. After nearly 40 years of marriage, Wade knows not to get involved when Janet's like this. Her out-of-place serenity (or is it confidence?) is disconcerting.

Mr. Jams looks at me, but I have nothing to offer. With heels dug in, he turns back to Janet.

"Yes."

We all take a breath as I pull out the dictionary. It's been a grueling two hours, and this is the deciding moment. "Let's see …" Thumbing through to the Xs, I find it:

"*Xenial* is a word. Sorry, Mr. Jams. Wade. Sorry, Me. Janet wins."

Janet's hands shoot up with a triumphant shout, her competitive appetite sated. The rest of us lick our wounds, something I've been doing for the past hour spent in last place. Janet and Mr. Jams want to pick things apart, find out who's been bluffing, who has the highest-scoring words.

Janet suddenly begins to giggle. "I have to confess something. When I challenged Mr. Jams and checked to see if his word *yabby* was real, I also checked to see if *xenial* was real. I cheated."

My jaw goes slack, my eyes come alive with incredulity. Wade begins shaking his head slowly, as though he's heard this confession before. Janet appears content, still high on the fact that she won the game, even as we protest the victory.

But on Planet Janet, the game is over. The victory remains.

While Janet sings "We Are the Champions" and Mr. Jams almost counters with "Another One Bites the Dust," I hit my mind's rewind button to recall the middle-aged Welsh couple who argued every night—in our presence—at dinner; Big Marcos with his terrible toilet aim and zero desire to clean up after himself; and the Frenchwoman who served us last year's mushy potatoes and onions at every meal. And in this moment, I definitively realize that age is but a number, that numerical years do not maturity make.

It's freeing, somehow, to know that this idea of adulthood I've always imagined—its rules, its expectations—is a sham. There's no mandatory role I must fulfill as I age. "Adulthood," it turns out, is just a thing people say to confuse young people. From now on, I'll craft my years how I wish, and no matter *what* happens, I'll at least not cheat at games.

In reality, it is all in good fun. The truth is, no matter how perturbed we are with Janet's admitted deception, she will be forgiven. Why? It has to do with her choosing us out of more than fifty applicants to housesit while she and Wade take a three-week trip to Singapore.

Their modern three-story home overlooks olive and orange groves and the glistening Mediterranean Sea. We'll care for their two sweet pups—a Jack Russell and a beagle—and be otherwise content with home-cooked meals (local leg of lamb, anyone?), picturesque strolls, drives through the countryside (in their '90s Land Rover), mild addictions to Downton Abbey, and other deliberate acts of guiltless leisure.

After six months work-exchanging in France, Israel, and Turkey, it's an amazing score—especially for housesit first-timers.

Will I end up missing work-exchange? Yes, a bit. But then again, it's coastal Greece and it's December, and I can think of no better way to spend the chilly holidays than in pure and simple vacation mode.

Chapter 12: Housesitting

Do you want to live in castles, beside olive groves, on a cattle ranch, or hidden in a log cabin in the woods? Then honey, housesitting is for you. I'm not talking about taking care of your neighbor's cat collection here; I'm talking about the hills of Tuscany, the flavors of Thailand, the beats of Morocco, and everything in between.

Housesitting is a very competitive option and is one of the best-kept secrets in the world of free travel, which is why this chapter was the most difficult to write. Naturally, the selfish traveler in me wants it to *remain* a secret. But, selfish me is locked away—we all deserve to travel for free!

The housesitting travel strategy may turn out to be your biggest key to unlocking the world-at-large. It's like staying in a "home-style" resort, but you have more autonomy and local cultural access, fewer on-site restaurants where you can stuff yourself silly, more upkeep and cleaning responsibilities, and, well ... it's *free*. While some long-term or highly prized housesits may ask you to pay the electric or water bills, it's rare; usually it's a perfectly symbiotic exchange!

Just think of it: all you have to do is get yourself there (see Chapter Five: Travel Hacking) and you'll have the comforts of home—a cozy bed, stocked kitchen, washer and dryer, and other creature comforts. It's almost too good to be true ... only *almost* because there is some caretaking involved, and yes, some people are hoarders.

Caretaking and hoarders aside, the trick is to be the "Chosen One." In fact, work-exchange, couchstays, housesitting, and most peer-sharing tools are dependent on you having a great personality and being able to prove it on an otherwise impersonal medium: the Internet.

MY TAKE: I can lead you to water, but I can't make you loveable. I know, I know. That's not how the expression goes. But that's how I roll. I can't teach you how to be personable (at least not in this book), but if you think you need some work on becoming that "Chosen One," start by reading Dale Carnegie's iconic work, **How to Win Friends and Influence People**. Free travel it is not, excellent read it is (and no, it's not as Machiavellian as it sounds). You're welcome.

Are we good to go? Let's take a deeper dive into housesitting. But please treat this information like it came from your grandma—with respect and like the treasure it is!

Is Housesitting for You?

With great housesitting gigs comes even greater responsibility! Seriously. You're taking care of someone's home, their most important investment, and their most valuable keepsakes. Add to that, you'll probably be caring for the love (or loves) of their life: a dog, cat, hamster, goat, or other creatures! It's no meager responsibility—one negative review by a homeowner means you can kiss your housesitting future goodbye at best and, at worst, find yourself in legal hot water.

If you're using housesitting as a daily, post-party crash pad or for day-long sightseeing excursions, it's probably not your best option. This is the travel option you choose only after you've flushed that stuff out of your system. This is how you adult in another country. If you're open to working your tourism in here and there around someone else's schedule, keep reading.

Not all housesits involve pet care. Some involve plant watering or pool maintenance, and others simply want someone around to keep ne'er-do-wells away. Either way, homeowners will expect you to spend chunks of time there during the day and to be present at night. Whatever the reason they need housesitting, it's up to you to respect it and stick to it.

So, is housesitting for you? Let's answer a few questions:

Can you stick to someone else's schedule?

The homeowner will outline all your responsibilities, which could include daily scheduled pet feedings, multiple plant waterings at specific times, and other random commitments. For example, one homeowner needed me home every day from 2 to 4 p.m. to accept a recurring postal delivery. What he was receiving remains a mystery to me! At any rate, don't be that guy. If you make an agreement, stick to it.

Would you be comfortable with different or questionable living conditions?

Cleanliness and organizational standards vary *hugely* from person to person. Consider them part of the adventure and keep your eye on the positive review prize. Get enough of those and you can be as choosy as you want with future jobs.

Are you a pet person and can you care for one like it's your own?

Most housesits are actually petsits, so it's important that you truly enjoy animals. Resist the temptation to put your desire to live or vacation elsewhere above the reality of what makes you happy on a day-to-day basis. Most pet owners treat pets like their children, and you're expected to rise to this level, even if it's weird (but not *that* weird). If yappy, overconfident, toy-sized dogs or needy, lazy lap cats drive you up the wall, don't claim otherwise.

Are you realistic about timing?

Like I mentioned in Chapter 4, housesit availability often depends on weather. When it's beautiful outside, homeowners typically want to be at home. Off-seasons and bad weather periods are when they try to get away. You'll still be able to find housesits nearly any time, you might just have to be more flexible about the destination.

Are you a troubleshooting ninja? Can you handle inconveniences on your own?

When homeowners are on vacation, they typically don't want to be bothered about house minutiae unless it's absolutely necessary. If you're not an independent, troubleshooting ninja, housesitting probably isn't for you.

Can you afford to get and stay there?

Obviously, you have to get to the house to do the housesitting job, so review *Part Two: Getting There* to make sure you can do it within budget.

Homeowners may or may not provide food or a *per diem*. Many leave a well-stocked kitchen and say "help yourself," but not all do this. When I apply to housesitting jobs, I usually allude to a well-stocked refrigerator in lieu of fees.

 KEEP YO' MONEY: Once you've garnered several positive reviews from housesitting jobs, you have the option to charge a fee. Remember that this is about exchange, though. I've only charged when I was on the fence about the housesit—if there weren't free transportation options nearby or if there was an immoderate amount of pet care, for example.

Do you want an inexpensive way to take a family trip?

Housesits are jackpots for families looking for affordable and manageable vacations instead of a hotel or the living room pull-out beds at the in-laws' house.

Are you between jobs, freelancing, or working remotely?

What better way to focus on profit and productivity than by not having to deal with living expenses?

Putting Yourself on the Market

The first thing to do is choose and register on a housesitting website. As with work-exchange sites, nearly all of them charge a yearly fee ranging from $20 to $80. Poke around each site and decide which one is best based on which has the most opportunities in your preferred destinations. When you've found the best match, register. *Voilà*!

My favorite site is TrustedHousesitters.com. Even though they're more expensive than most ($119 yearly, or less if you find the registration discounts they frequently offer), their layout is easy to navigate and they typically have the most options. The pricey registration fee helps to ensure a higher level of professionalism, security, and mutually beneficial experiences for everyone involved. Plus, that yearly fee can easily cover the cost of lodging in an Airbnb or hostel!

Here are the websites that provide the best overall selection of housesitting opportunities:

Worldwide:

TrustedHousesitters.com
HouseCarers.com
HomeAway.com
MindMyHouse.com
Nomador.com

United States:

HouseSittersAmerica.com

Europe:

HouseSitMatch.com

Australia:

AussieHouseSitters.com.au

New Zealand:

KiwiHouseSitters.co.nz/

UK:

HouseSittersUK.co.uk

Creating a Profile

After registering with a housesitting website, it's time to create an outstanding profile. Trust is a huge deciding factor in housesitting, so it's important to be personable, honest, and transparent when creating your profile. Many sites provide the option to pay a small fee for a background check, and while I've yet to do it, it does help give homeowners peace of mind.

Here's **what you should include**:

⇨ A bit about you (where you grew up, what you studied, areas of experience, hobbies, etc.).

⇨ If you're pet-friendly. Do you have a pet? What kind? What's its name?

⇨ Why you've chosen housesitting, why it meshes with your lifestyle (viewers will be curious—are you a freelancer, retired?), and why you'd be good at it.

⇨ Relevant experience (animal care, gardening, pool care, carpentry, etc.).

⇨ Other qualities or information that makes you stand out or more useful.

Below is a sample profile based on what I've used. While I err on the side of T.M.I. (too much information), I've known some housesitters who provide the bare minimum and still have great success scoring jobs.

Sample Housesitting Profile

Hi there! I'm a current nomad (but Georgia-born) writer and petsitter who loves travel! Despite an International Business degree, I prefer quiet days at home writing and cooking to business suits and boardrooms!

My writing profession lends a very flexible schedule where I can see the world through housesitting, and since I can't commit to having pets of my own (yet), I get to have an extended pet family all over the world!

If you could be a fly on the wall while I housesit, you would see lots of cooking, reading, writing, singing, and yoga. I also like jogging and long walks—pets are welcome to join! I'm experienced with garden and pool maintenance, and I certainly don't shy away from general home upkeep.

I've cared for dogs, cats, llamas, alpacas, sheep, chickens, lizards, horses, cows, and more, in settings such as high elevations, deep snow, complete isolation, busy cities, and everything in-between! I believe it's extremely important to care for homes the way *you* expect, not the way *I* want to do things ... that's the whole point of finding someone trustworthy, right?

I grew up with lots of travel and very much prefer "living" somewhere versus running around playing tourist. To me, a "vacation" is more about really *living* somewhere for a while.

How will I treat your pets? I take a family member approach, learning each one's individual personality with patience and empathy. I welcome detailed care instructions and/or special needs cases and take care to understand your pet's needs, temperament, and any medication requirements, and also to continue the routine to which they're accustomed.

Whether or not you have pets, I hope you've picked up that I'm an honest gal who simply hopes for a safe and fun exchange with you, your home, and your pet family!

Be yourself and let it shine! A sense of humor, self-assurance, and independence are big pluses for most homeowners. Ultimately, express your desire to work with them to create a symbiotic experience for you both. Remember, your personality won't appeal to everyone, but it will appeal to the right ones—that's what really matters.

The Picture

The digital dating singles will understand this: How often do you look at a profile without a photo and think, "Oh yeah! What a clever description! *NEXT*!"? The same can be said for your housesitting profile.

You could describe yourself as the Mother Theresa of housesitters, but homeowners will probably skip you entirely if they can't see you—perhaps even from several angles.

Aim for 5 to 10 snapshots, max out at 20. Show yourself in a variety of settings, smiling (obviously) and doing active and relevant things, like happily petting animals, gardening, fixing stuff, and other visuals that present you in a desirable light.

Videos and Testimonials

If the website offers the option to upload a short introductory video about yourself, go for it! Just one or two minutes is all it takes to share your energy and communicate how responsible and reliable you are. Homeowners love videos. Bonus points for subtitles in the host's language!

Never played a leading role in a self-made promo video? Any computer, laptop, tablet, or smartphone with a decent video camera will do. Just **follow these tips**:

↬ Record during the day.

↬ Avoid standing with your back to a window (the backlight will darken your moneymaker—your face!).

↬ Stand facing a window for natural lighting.

↬ Record yourself from the waist up, but no face close-ups—that's just a bit intense. Plus, a face close-up means you're holding the camera selfie-style, and that tends to look unprofessional.

↬ Use a friend, tripod, or other rigging to hold the camera steady.

↬ Dress to impress.

↬ Situate yourself in a calm, organized setting—no cluttered backgrounds.

Reviews are your best friend

Reach out to friends to write good character references or house and pet sitter reviews for you (if you've actually been a caretaker for them). This will be crucial since you won't yet have website-certified references from past jobs. When we were only 26, Mr. Jams and I beat out 50 other applicants despite having no site-verified references. Luckily, we had three external reviews from friends. It was a spectacular score for a modern three-story home on the coast of Greece.

If the website you've chosen doesn't allow non-site-verified reviews, include them in your bio's body text. Some sites discourage this, but because I don't see a downside to it, I say give it a shot. The benefits of testimonials are just too valuable to forego.

 KEEP YO' MONEY: Going with a housesitting website helps add legitimacy and professionalism to the experience, but if you want to avoid these upfront costs, build a personalized sitter website (Wordpress, SquareSpace, etc.) and post it on websites like Yelp, YellowPages, Craigslist, and other sites for locals.

Finding and Applying

The search functions of housesitting sites vary, but usually you'll start by specifying dates and viewing available results as a list or on a map. Time is of the essence since the fastest responders often get priority, so make sure you've signed up to receive email notifications of new listings. You can usually choose to receive them in a daily digest, in real time as they're listed, and filtered for your desired destinations.

Listings themselves are all across the board. Some homeowners may bizarrely only post a picture of their pet or a selfie and add a few lines explaining that Pookie needs someone to take care of her for a while. Most, though, give more than enough information, even telling you how many times per day you'll need to scoop the kitty litter box.

When you see a job you're interested in, apply as quickly as possible with a feeler message (remember feeler messages in Chapter 11?) to express intent and request more information as early as possible.

Here's a brief feeler message to give you an idea the basic structure you can follow:

Sample Housesitting Feeler Message

Heya Tommy,

I know you'll probably have lots of applications to sift through, so thanks for reading mine! Spending time with Barks and Mewy in your slice of Belgium sounds like a real treat. I do my best to take care of your pets and property in exactly the way you designate—there's nothing better than coming back to happy animals and a home the way you left it!

A bit about me: I grew up in Georgia and worked in car sales before this, but have been traveling and living through housesitting for the past year. It's a great lifestyle that enables me to see the world without emptying my bank account! I now work remotely as a sales rep for an online pet store, so since I work from home, I can give all the cuddles and play time that Barks and Mewy need!

Please feel free to call or write if you'd like to chat more, and in the meantime, I'd love to see more photos of the home if you're interested (this is a standard question I've learned to ask due to some "surprises" I've encountered in the past!) or we could do a Skype video chat and home tour?

Thanks for your consideration!

Betsy

The first message won't mean you're committing to anything, but it will hopefully get your foot in the door. Some homeowners get so overwhelmed by responses within the first day that only the first five or ten get read at all—fewer if they are content with the first few applicants.

Every person is seeking something different in a housesitter; write to each one with a mind toward what is said and perhaps *not* said in their listing. Your intuition might tell you that they seem pretty darn nervous about leaving their stuff with a stranger, so show empathy and confidence in your ability to protect their home or love their pet. Others simply want a trustworthy, reliable, and independent person who won't call every time the sink drips or Pookie seems sad. In this case, show yourself to be relaxed, self-sufficient and adult-like.

Most importantly, try to arrange a phone or Skype interview. The sooner they put a voice (and hopefully a face) to your name and profile, the higher your odds of getting the gig. A conversation is great on both ends to get a feel for the people involved and if you'll be compatible. Video calls are also ideal for a tour of the home. Yay technology!

I *really* advise getting a good look of the house before committing. Environment often influences mood and behavior, so if you prefer a certain aesthetic—for example, natural lighting and uncluttered spaces—don't compromise. Be true to your preferences. You may find yourself in an apartment smack in the middle of bustling Paris, but it might also reflect *ambiance à la crackhouse*. It's probably just not the best choice.

If you've found that unicorn and your gut is telling you that this is the one—even before getting a good look at the space—let them know you're ready to commit. Otherwise, ask for the digital tour to get a better feel for the home and its vibe. If they can't figure that out, request more photos or follow-up conversations. The following is what I usually say to a homeowner—it essentially puts the blame on my professional life if I decide the house is a no-go:

"Would you mind sending additional photos of the home's interior like the kitchen, bedrooms, or work spaces? I work from home (which is why housesitting is a dream!) but I'm really terrible at focusing sometimes, so it'll help me to know what the house is like. Thank you!"

Discussing the Job

If the homeowner responds with interest, congrats! Respond quickly and take some time to get to know them. It's not just about being chosen, it's about ensuring the gig is mutually beneficial. Ask relevant questions about their expectations, past experience with housesitting, if any, and if there's anything else you should know about staying there.

MY TAKE: Housesitting is a symbiotic exchange based on trust. If a homeowner seems overly suspicious of having strangers take care of their house, this might be the red flag you need to say no thanks. I usually run from anyone who feels the need to micromanage with daily calls or video chats, and especially if they have a camera recording the home's interior!

You haven't yet scored the job, so don't ask *too* many questions and risk seeming demanding or needy. You should, however, **consider obtaining the following information** well in advance if it's not detailed in their listing:

⇨ What are the exact travel dates?

⇨ Do I need to arrive early to learn the ropes?

⇨ What are my specific responsibilities—yard work, mail collection, pet care routines (meals, exercise, health care, etc.)?

⇨ What's the area/community like—quiet, peaceful, active, loud, depends on the day or time?

⇨ How often will you want updates on the home or pets?

⇨ What are my transportation options around the area—spare car, bicycle, public transportation, walking?

⇨ What's the best way to get to their home from my arrival point?

⇨ What are the neighbors like?

⇨ What are the house's issues/quirks I need know about—haunted-but-friendly, limited hot water, loose bottom stair?

 INSIDER INFO: Most (not all!) homeowners will offer you a ride to and from their home. Since they're obviously going somewhere, offer to return the favor if you have a car or if they're okay with you using theirs.

Booking the Job

Once you both agree to the housesit, it's time to iron out the finer details. Most websites allow homeowners to officially note you as the upcoming sitter, though it's not required. I seldom have more confirmation than a verbal agreement or an email. Hosts often request that you arrive a day or two early so they can show you the ropes and get to know you in person—that should be more than enough time.

As you prepare, request that certain relevant information be put in writing. A physical copy of important information often comes in handy. The items below are **ideal inclusions**:

⇨ Maintenance issues/requirements

⇨ Homeowner's contact information (primary and alternate)

⇨ Location of necessities like cleaning products, circuit breaker, extra sheets, fire extinguishers

⇨ A list or schedule of required responsibilities for home, property, pets, and/or appliances

⇨ Ground rules (noise levels among neighbors; day visitors and/or overnight guests; off-limit rooms; forbidden items such as certain food, alcohol, or rings to rule the world; maximum time away from the home; etc.)

⇨ Garbage and recycling schedules

⇨ Relevant area maps if not easily found online

⇨ Wi-Fi login information

⇨ Postal collection (box keys, important items to watch for, expected deliveries)

⇨ If relevant, how to address worst-case weather-related scenarios like tornadoes or flooding

⇨ If providing a car, ensure the insurance policy allows a guest driver

⇨ Request copies of warranty and insurance information if they aren't in the car

⇨ Smoke and carbon monoxide detector locations and functionality (ask if batteries are new or need replacing)

⇨ Fireplace safety and upkeep if use is permitted

⇨ Alarm/security system details (codes, operation, window/door contacts)

⇨ Request a spare key be left with a neighbor or in a safe hiding spot. If the homeowner is uncomfortable with this, hide the house key in a lockable space like a storage shed, then hide the shed key somewhere outside the house. Double protection!

 ACHTUNG! One homeowner asked me to arrive five days in advance, but we settled on three. After arrival, I quickly realized that he'd really just wanted someone to keep him company. With most jobs, one to two days prior is plenty of time, but one time, due to a mix-up in flight planning, Mr. Jams and I ended up staying with our first housesit hosts for *five* days before they left. Despite a 50-year age difference, we had a blast! We even stayed with them for three days after they got back. Plus, they cooked, took us sightseeing and out to eat, and wouldn't let us pay for any of it!

Information and Questions for a Housesit with Pets

⇨ A description of the pets' characters, habits, and particular fears they may have (thunder, mail carriers, cucumbers, housesitters, etc.)

⇨ Relevant ongoing or past issues (health, aggression, ability to levitate, etc.)

⇨ Veterinarian or animal hospital contact/location

⇨ Location of pet necessities—food, kitty litter, favorite toys, etc.

⇨ List or schedule of required duties, appointments, and medication

⇨ What to do in the event of worst-case scenarios (like an escape or drastic change in behavior)

Some homeowners want to maintain light correspondence until the job begins; this helps them feel reassured they made the right choice with you—the complete stranger—caring for their worldly possessions. Others stay silent about logistics until it's closer to the arrival date. That's okay too. Either way, you'll be beautifully prepared because of this little book right here, so start packing!

What to Do Upon Arrival

I can't tell you what your arrival will be like, but I can say that it might be … interesting. Some people are completely relaxed with the situation, some radiate tension like a priest in a brothel. It's fine—they're probably stressed about their trip or a little worried about leaving everything with you (remember—the stranger?). Do the little gift thing (remember—the chocolate or souvenir?) and just relax.

Treat the housesitting job with all the respect, responsibility, and maturity of a real job. Take the time with the homeowner to review important topics and take notes once they start giving you the grand tour. And really, pay attention—things mentioned in passing might be commonplace knowledge to *them*, but news to you.

Sometimes I'm in such a state of excitement toward my new digs that I miss important information, even something as simple as how to run a washing machine (those things have minds of their own!). Ask questions—the homeowner will feel more assured and it will prevent unwanted calls if things happen.

 PRO TIP: If the homeowner wishes to leave a room locked, suggest that they leave the key in a sealed envelope to be opened in case of an emergency (like a pipe leak or broken window within the room).

If you arrive early, you'll often be asked to have dinner as the homeowner's guest, so remember to offer help prepare and clean up. If you're a housesitting family (two or more), the homeowner will *probably* still offer to cook dinner, but it might be easier to take your unit out for dinner or prepare things on your own. Offering to cook dinner for the homeowner would be a lovely gesture, too (plus, remember what I said about getting good reviews)!

The days leading up to a trip can be pretty hectic, so give the homeowner space if it seems they need it. Some may want to play tour guide around town and some will want you to leave them alone so they can finish getting organized.

During the Housesit

Now the real fun starts! Introvert that I am, I always breathe a sigh of relief once the homeowner departs. Time to try on a new lifestyle!

Here are a few **things to remember** to ensure you have a successful housesitting gig:

⇨ Keep in touch—the peace of mind you offer homeowners with regular updates is priceless and will go far to score you a good review. Ask in advance how often you should update them. Most homeowners love daily correspondence when furbabies are involved, though some will prefer a *no news is good news* approach. When you do reach out, score extra points by sending happy photos of the pet.

⇨ Lock doors and windows when you're away.

⇨ Keep electric and water usage low. Close doors of unoccupied rooms, turn off lights, and adjust the thermostat to normal levels—especially when you're away.

⇨ Don't leave mail on the street or in the mailbox; this is a signal to burglars that the house is unoccupied and one of the very reasons you were brought on to housesit in the first place, silly!

⇨ Don't end the housesit with the fridge and cupboards bare, even if you were told to help yourself. Nobody wants to come home from traveling only to turn around for a grocery store run. You don't have to stock up, but some replaced snacks and enough food for a meal is perfect. Feeling extra charitable? Have a prepared meal waiting for them when they get back. (Reviews, people, *reviews!*)

⇨ Always keep the home in tip-top shape, ideally as clean as it was left for you, if not cleaner. You never know when a friend or family member will pop in to ("innocently") say hello, then pop back out … to report to the homeowner.

TALES FROM THE ROAD: My favorite housesitting experience was in a rustic but renovated three-story Tuscan stone farmhouse. The owner was a writer as well and her home had a simple, cozy writing nook downstairs by the kitchen.

A spartan middle floor contained the master bedroom, living room, and office, and the sunlit third-story room overlooking the surrounding hills and valleys was like a mystical overlord's watchtower. This was where the harvested fleece of five alpacas (under my care) was loomed. It was also the space in which I secluded myself with a book and my thoughts.

Each morning, I crossed the cobblestones to the tiny town's local cafe for an *espresso lungo*. And every afternoon, her two dogs walked me up the mountain in the backyard. It's also where I laid the foundation for this very book!

Legal Considerations

Homeowners and sitters often may settle on a verbal agreement for the housesit. That being said, a written housesitting agreement is always a good and demonstrably responsible idea in case legal issues arise.

If going with this option, ask whether the homeowner is comfortable with you drafting something (think twice if they say no!). Once you send it over for review, ask if there's anything they'd like adjusted or added. Agreements can be as lengthy or short as you like, but **consider including**:

⇨ Homeowner's name
⇨ Home address
⇨ Dates of the housesit
⇨ Name of housesitter
⇨ Dates covered by the agreement
⇨ Terms of the housesit (home occupancy period, whether other guests/animals are allowed, etc.)
⇨ Written confirmation that the agreement is not a lease or legally binding
⇨ Any expected payments/reimbursements from either the sitter or homeowner

There is an excellent **printable draft agreement** from MindMy-House.com.[3] Use it in its entirety or reproduce it to fit your specific situation.

If you plan to housesit or petsit often, consider getting bonded and insured for personal coverage. Let's hope you're never accused of theft or animal neglect (please don't give reasons to be accused!), but if that happens, it's best to have coverage.

Legality aside, the most important thing to remember about housesitting is to enjoy yourself! It's an unparalleled opportunity to relax, work on your favorite hobbies, and see new places. It's also a lifestyle—certain sitters have been mortgage- and rent-free for decades through housesitting. Whether long or short term, it's prime time to escape your normal and live a different life for a while.

---

[3] https://www.mindmyhouse.com/assets/downloads/house_sitting_agreement.pdf

Interlude:
Four Tales From the Road

Among all my free accommodation memories, I have the best from the couchstay community. I've been cautious about my choice of hosts and have never encountered anyone untoward, but don't get me wrong—the weirdos are out there, men and women alike! With careful planning and an open mind, I've had only rewarding experiences. Like what, you ask?

1. One of my first couchstays took place in my early 20s on a roadtrip with my friend Carson through Napa Valley, California. I was managing a specialty food shop in Jackson, Wyoming and had the convenient excuse of needing to source wine for the shop's nascent restaurant. Our host, Emily, was living with her parents, so we scored a five-star sleep in the home's plush guest bedroom before the next day's vineyard-hopping.

We awoke to the smell of mom-cooked pancakes and the good news that Emily wanted to join us as designated driver. Deal! Careening through the vineyard-flanked hills, we arrived to our first winery only to find that my status as a restaurant rep meant all the tastings were free. Free wine! Free driver! Free cozy bed! *L'chaim*, y'all!

2. Another unforgettable couchstay experience in Ephesus, Turkey, was with a solitary middle-aged man who gave up his bed for Mr. Jams and me while he slept on the couch. He loved having guests (something I presumed to be an infrequent occurrence) and could barely keep from putting on his proverbial tour guide hat while hammering out questions in broken but bold English about life in America. And hey, I can totally forgive the guy for using my computer to have Skype sex with an Internet call girl. He had a good heart. (Delete that chat history, y'all!)

3. In the French town of Brillat St. Savin, our host, Margot, a physical therapist in her late 30s, became a fast friend to my sister and me when we showed up with a bottle of rosé. We ate a home-cooked dinner and talked long into the night about being independent women in our 30s (*ahem*, who run the world?).

The coastal town's rambunctious summer festival began the next day, so we kicked things off with fresh grilled sardines and French fries (of course!) at Margot's brother's local seafood restaurant. As afternoon fell, Margot led us through endless cobblestone alleys to the best bars and liveliest concerts lasting well into the night. We ate fried fish, danced Riverdance-esque jigs, and even met the town mayor, who stayed on as our enthusiastically drunk sidekick for the night. We partied with the mayor, y'all!

4. My host in Genoa, Italy (a gorgeous psychotherapist, I might add) picked me up at the train station, and within the hour I was on the back of his motorcycle, zooming up a mountain through low, all-encompassing white clouds. Winding our way down, we sped to a nearby beach where I swam in the Mediterranean for my very first time.

On his free nights, he led me through the ancient streets of that labyrinthine city, drinking local libations and devouring legendary pastas. During the day, he left me his spare set of apartment keys so I could explore on my own, coming and going as I pleased. I was living like a local in Genoa—the city of pesto, focaccia, and of course, Genoa salami. *Ragazza genovese*, y'all!

These are just a few of many times my couchstay hosts went above and beyond for no other reason than pure, honest-to-goodness kindness. As a host in Jackson Hole, I loved taking couchstayers hiking through the stunning Rocky Mountains, rafting on the Snake River, dancing until all hours in a mountain valley overlooking the Teton mountain range, and much, much more. I may be introverted, but when travel magic kicks in, I get a sudden urge to share amazing experiences with good people and new friends.

But for now, storytime is over. Let's learn how to find your *own* free-wine-and-cheesing, french-festivaling, motorcycle-riding, and phone-sex-free fantastic couchstay!

Chapter 13: Couchstays

It's fitting that I begin writing this chapter after hanging up with my parents—both in their 60s—who have just said goodbye to their first-ever couchstay guest. Was it successful? Indeed! Did I orchestrate it? You betcha!

Suffice it to say dear ol' mom and dad are now totally psyched to be couchstay hosts for life. And that is the spirit of good travel, is it not? To bring us together while we wander apart.

I've been in the P2P couchstay community since I left university, and I'll use it as long as I'm still traveling. No doubt some of my best travel experiences and dearest friends have emerged through completely free couchstays with strangers.

Couchstays provide free lodging all over the world, and hosts often like to serve as local guides. You'd think that travelers would jump at this opportunity, yet in the years I've used it, there's been zero decrease in the raised eyebrows I get upon explaining this concept to the unfamiliar.

This is how it usually plays out:

1) Person asks about my travel lodging

2) I tell Person about staying on a stranger's couch (or in their spare bedroom)

3) Fear and/or disgust grows in Person's eyes

4) Line of questioning ensues: "Wait! Do you even know this person? How do you know they're safe? How are you so 'la-di-da' and trusting?! Are you sure you wanna do this?!"

This is a book, so you can't experience my "sigh of meh" or witness my "rolling eyes of whatever." Couchstays are not nightclub hookups or anonymous Craigslist posts. Vetted couchstay websites go to great lengths to attract and promote sincere and safe members—the system works. Peer reviewing keeps bad seeds at bay, kind of like upvoting the quality stuff on Reddit or rating and reviewing on Yelp.

Yes, you stay with strangers. *No,* the risk is no greater than that taken each time you ride in a car. *Yes,* the rewards far outweigh the risks—and bear in mind, the risks are mutual; hosts are also taking gambles on their occupants being good people.

The following pages will help reduce even further any risks and hesitations associated with couchstaying. But if you're still nervous about hosting or couchstaying after reading this chapter, all I can say is this: Try it. Try it *one* time and you may just become a life-long couchstayer.

From someone who's been a host and been hosted all over the world, I've learned one essential truth: the differences we perceive in other cultures (often through news and hearsay) are never as great as our fundamental similarities. Most people, wherever their origin, are kind, curious, and fun-loving at heart. There's no better place to discover this than from the vantage of someone else's couch.

Choosing a Platform

The big dog of couchstays is most definitely Couchsurfing.com. Back in the day, Couchsurfing.com was more like a free secret club for travelers, but as it's grown, there's more need for regulation. I hate to say it, but it seems that more people use couchstays now with no regard for its true sharing spirit and culture, often treating host homes like a hotel with maid service.

Another downside to Couchsurfing.com is its popularity; hosts in big cities sometimes get so inundated with requests that they grow overwhelmed and won't respond to anything at all. Check out the alternative sites listed below. While they won't have Couchsurfing.com's user base, the users they do have will often be more receptive to your communication since it's usually quieter overall.

Best Couchstay Resources:

Couchsurfing.com
HospitalityClub.org
Servas.org
LGHEI.org
   (for the LGBT community)
Staydu.com
BeWelcome.org

WarmShowers.org
   (popular with cyclists)
Trustroots.org
   (for backpackers and
   hitchhikers)
GlobalFreeloaders.com

Before we get into how to increase your odds of being accepted as a couchstayer on a big site like Couchsurfing.com, let's first focus on setting up your profile so you have any chance at all. If you've read the work-exchange and housesitting sections in this book, it's essentially the same song and dance. The advantage is that you don't have to highlight your great work ethic or animal care knowledge. You just have to prove you'll be a good housemate for the duration of your stay.

Create that Profile

This book is for the traveler, so the following information is for guests more than hosts. Membership requirements are usually the same for both, but it works to your advantage to put yourself out there as a host as well. This is a good way to accumulate reviews from guests, and knowing what it's like to be a good host will certainly make you a better guest.

Once you choose your platforms and register, create an in-depth profile with detailed responses in all possible sections (favorite music, movies genres, etc.). Introduce yourself with a creative paragraph about your background, interests, and why you're interested in couchstays. Provide several photos of yourself in a variety of circumstances.

 ACHTUNG! Be extremely wary of host profiles riddled with too many selfies! In some instances, this has been a way for hosts to use couchstays to facilitate hookups or other less-than-gracious endeavors.

I use the Pareto Principle: there should be at least 80% "normal" photos.

Your profile is your handshake—convey trust, safety, and the ways you and potential hosts could be compatible. If that handshake's flimsy at the outset, chances of success are low. Similarly, if a possible host has a crummy profile, they're not doing their part to convey trust. Don't waste your time!

Be yourself to better your chances of finding a host with whom you're compatible. For example, a strict vegan might not want to stay with a game hunter. Outspoken Bernie defender? Probably best to avoid a South-Will-Rise-Again-Trumpie.

More often than not, you'll end up staring at the ceiling wondering how best to describe yourself. And sometimes it's the tiniest detail you decided to add at the last minute that seals the deal, like your favorite author or band. Try to put yourself in the shoes of a host. What kind of profile would catch your eye when looking for an ideal couchstay guest?

Earning Reviews

Peer reviews are your friends on couchstay websites. This is probably one of the best ways to know which hosts are the best hosts. You can determine safety levels, degree of comfort, personality compatibilities, and many other factors you look for in a prospective couchstay host.

But the truth is, you probably won't find many *overtly* negative reviews if the host ... sucks. Reviewers don't want to seem like a-holes—it's a blessing and a curse. Still, if you read between the lines (or if the review is really short), you can often decipher what someone is *truly* saying (or not saying) about their experience.

For example, consider the following two actual couchstay host reviews:

⇨ *"Jessica is a fantastic host! Very polite, tidy, and interesting. Great conversationalist! We went to her family cookout and had a great time hearing her stories and sharing ours. We also went into Barcelona together to check out the MNAC, and afterwards she cooked a fabulous dinner! Hopefully we will see each other again :)"*

⇨ *"Mike was a nice and very talkative host. Good luck with everything!"*

Which host would you contact? Jessica or Mike? From where I'm sitting, Jessica seems like the perfect host, and Mike's reviewer sounds like they spent the duration listening to Mike blab his head off. However, in context, if Mike has lots of other positive reviews, perhaps this particular guest was just clueless, super antisocial, or having a bad week.

Here are some **sample reviews with hints** about what you might expect in a host. This is particularly helpful if you identify as either an introvert (like me) or an extrovert:

1. "She's home a lot, so you'll have plenty of time to get to know each other."
   Translation → Stay away if you want to be left alone. Have at it if you're traveling alone and craving human interaction.

2. "If you want a tour guide, he's your guy."
   Translation → Solo explorers need not apply, but perfect if you want someone to show you the sites.

3. "She has an exciting life. I felt like I was back in college at a frat house."
   Translation → Party animal! Proceed with caution if you value peace and quiet.

4. "Lots of friends often dropped in."
   Translation → A great way for embedding with the locals. Not a great way to keep to yourself.

Not attempting to garner reviews is a bad idea for a community based on social exchange. I believe that reviews are so important they should be at the top of your list of where to get the truth about a couchstay host.

Since they're so important, try to gather them for your *own* profile ASAP. Most sites even allow simple character references from other members if you haven't yet hosted or been a guest. The odds are that you already know members (at least on Couchsurfing.com), so ask around to find them and offer to do a review exchange—it's a back-scratching thing.

Another great way to get better acquainted with the couchstay community is to attend events hosted by the couchstay website, like concerts, pub crawls, and recreational sports leagues. Get involved! Then you can connect with other members and get references. Some social circles are built entirely upon local couchstay members. If there aren't any events, create one!

Don't despair if you live in a small town without many other couchstay members. A well-made profile (combined with a great message, which we'll soon discuss) is still likely to get an eventual request or a place on a couch. If you have no reviews, point viewers to other ways that show you're a "real" person like a social media account, online videos, or your website.

Crafting the Asking

One more step ensures a couchstay for you: an amazing ask. The rule of any sales pitch applies: if you don't have a good hook, they won't bite. Craft your message showing you've thoroughly read the host's profile— this *highly* increases your odds of acceptance. Remember that hosts take a risk when accepting strangers into their home—don't take that lightly.

Because of oversaturation in bigger cities, you may have to send anywhere from 10 to 30 requests a day to receive a positive response. Many hosts (especially in urban centers) get inundated with boilerplate bulk requests. Of *course* they won't spend time considering a request if it doesn't stand out. 30 requests take up to two hours per sitting, but instead of paying $70 a night to stay in an Airbnb or a motel, I spend two hours doing the work to then stay somewhere for free for three nights. That's like getting paid $210 for two hours' work!

Here's a great message request I received from a couchstay friend named Maverick. He has over 300 positive reviews on Couchsurfing. com and is an amazing representative of the spirit of couchstay culture:

"Aye-Oh Miss Meggan, hope all is phenomenal in your world as you read this and that the dates of this request might match your availability so we can swap stories in the not-too-distant future.

You should know there are several reasons why I am asking for a couch from you when there are a handful of hosts in the Santa Fe area. For one, I like that we both have a background in the entertainment industry in Hollywood, yet more so that we have moved beyond it for other dreams. Also, we both appear to be funny foodies. I too offer metaphorical ears to hosts and guests on the regular; it's lovely how people can open up to a 'stranger' so quickly and thoroughly. Lastly, worth mentioning at this moment, I love that we seem to have a completely synced view on how to host with an 'I'm not your tour-guide' approach and an appreciation for guests showing they appreciate the hospitality offered in a tangible way.

So, I'm messaging to inquire about your availability to host me and a road trip companion with whom I'll be rambling through. Regardless, I'd love to invite you to connect with us while we are in town. If you ever head to Vegas, Venice Beach, or Yosemite (the three places I bounce among) let's chat about a rendezvous!

No matter if we connect now, later, or never, I wish you only the best with your CouchSurfing experience."

Now *that* is an ask! I knew I'd accept within the first few lines. **Here's why:**

1. He used my name and location at the outset. So he's read at least some of my profile and didn't do a quick copy/paste.
2. The intro, and most of the ask itself, is entertaining.
3. He gave me *three* reasons why he was specifically requesting me as host. Now it's confirmed: he's read my whole profile. He wouldn't know these details otherwise.
4. He closed the request in a friendly way—almost as if we grew up together. And like a good friend, he'd love to reciprocate if able.

Requests like Maverick's are, sadly, few and far between, but hopefully that will change. To summarize, using Maverick as our paradigm, here's **what to mention in your ask**:

1. Greet the host *by name*.
2. Use a creative and entertaining hook at the top.

 MY TAKE: I make it very apparent at the top of my profile that I'm pretty hands-off as a host and couchstayer, but that I'm open to grabbing a meal or a drink every so often. This is a preemptive tactic to weed out those with whom I may not get along so well, but it's also protecting my introvert ideals. The boundary is set early and potential hurt feelings are spared. That said, some of the best times I've had are when I connect with the host or guest!

3. Tell them about yourself and your travel plans.

4. Describe your ideal couchstay situation and set expectations early. Do you want solitude or company? Are you looking for a travel buddy or self-discovery? Can you handle home cookin' or is eating out your preference?

5. Find and mention secret words. Many hosts will incorporate a secret word in their profiles to make sure you've read it to the end. Never forget to incorporate it in your ask, or you can kiss that opportunity goodbye. It may sound silly or drastic, but it's a good way to weed out lazy template asks.

The Couchstay Experience

Couchstays involve two (or more) strangers suddenly and intentionally living together—it might feel strange the first time. It might take time to navigate. But after you've done it once, it starts to feel pretty normal.

Here are some **keys to remember** when couchstaying:

1. Show up with a gift like candy, wine, or a quirky souvenir from home. You're staying for free, and they're probably *losing* money from higher utility bills.

2. Be in tune with your host's mood—unlike you, they're not traveling. Perhaps work, friends, love life, or other things are keeping them preoccupied. Or perhaps they want to spend time with you. Be considerate of their mood and schedule. When in doubt, ask.

3. Be *extremely* fastidious about cleaning up after yourself. Follow the "leave no trace" rule each morning, especially if sleeping in a communal space. Assume your hosts are neat freaks, even it's obvious they aren't—they may have double standards when it comes to guests.

4. Go the extra mile and do some communal cleaning. When guests help me with kitchen cleanup, they can usually stay indefinitely. I've also kicked out an oblivious guest who didn't clean up after herself and her furniture-ravaging dog.

5. Tell the host your plans for the day so you can coordinate in case of locked doors. Never expect the host to adjust their schedule around yours—this is just something to deal with. If you're lucky, they'll offer a set of keys or tell you where the spare is hidden, but it's not guaranteed.

6. If keys aren't provided, plan accordingly. You may have to leave while the host is out, so pack a bag of supplies, like food and a phone charger. Keep your host's contact information with you in case of an emergency.

> **RETHINK IT:** *Don't* ask about the availability of a spare key. Let your host offer it when they're comfortable with a complete stranger in their home. Trust is a precious thing—don't ruin it with pressured demands and expectations.

Flexibility and openness are imperative because every host and home is different. Just be honest and awesome. It is up to you to respect the wishes of your host and be an outstanding couchstay guest! Read profiles thoroughly; discuss expectations even more thoroughly. Most of all, enjoy forming memories and lasting friendships the world over.

Chapter 14: But Wait! There's More!

The trifecta of work-exchange, housesitting, and couchstays will see you through a lifetime of free travel, but do you think I'm gonna stop there? *Please.* Other free accommodation options may be a bit more off the beaten track, but that doesn't make them less fabulous or easy. And just in case you decide to ball out on a paid room some night, I'm going to tell you how to save on *that*, too!

Warmshowers.org

Warmshowers is like couchstays for outdoorsy people, namely bicyclists, and it has no affiliation with R. Kelly. It's grown in popularity to accommodate all sorts of travelers who are happy to camp under the stars, but you'll have the most luck if you're at least a fan of cycling. Hosts provide a backyard (usually free, sometimes for a small fee) in which you can set up camp, but if you're lucky they might offer you a guest bedroom or their couch. Some also give access to kitchens, bathrooms, and showers, oh my!

Camping

Camping is often free, a great way to get in tune with your inner granola, and an even better way to meet other grain-fed travelers. Oh, and don't forget you're saving lots of cash by cooking for yourself.

It's pretty easy to find free campsites with a websearch for your intended destination, but there's always the option to camp wherever you can find a secretive spot (roadsides, secluded fields, etc.). My friend Carson couldn't find a cheap, last-minute spot to hunker down in Santiago, Chile before a kayaking trip. It was dark, and she was tired after a late-night bus arrival, so she found a field, rolled herself up in a kayaking tarp, and slept. The next day, she realized she'd been sleeping in a cemetery! It *was* free, though. And quiet.

If you'd prefer to rest among the living, peer-sharing websites like Campspace.com and Warmshowers.org allow hosts to offer their private backyards for free or a small charge. Often this includes access to a shower, use of a kitchen, and at least a high five from your host.

Remember to account for the cost of actually getting to campsites. Unless you're cycling, you may need to hire a car or a ride-share if public transport won't get you there. Finally, be vigilant about checking weather forecasts, and remember that the extra camping gear will obviously add lots of weight to your already-heavy travel bag—there is a price for comfort.

 ACHTUNG! I'm talking to my female readers here . . . mostly. Camping may not be your safest option. Read host reviews if you're staying in backyards, and look for well-populated public campgrounds. And pack mace. Beautiful, beautiful mace.

Wild Camping

Like Mr. Greenfield mentioned in Chapter 9, virtually all BLM land in North America is free. Check to see if your destination has something similar, but know that several countries allow camping on any public lands. Called Wild Camping, the rules are usually to (1) ditch your vehicle, (2) keep out of sight, (3) clean up after yourself, and (4) be responsible (don't burn the world down, ya ninny!). The UK, Ireland, Scandinavia, Spain, Portugal, Estonia, Turkey, Mongolia, Iceland, and Kyrgyzstan are particularly tolerant of getting wild.

Best International Camping Resources:

Many countries have region-specific camping websites. Find them with an online search.

Campspace.com
Warmshowers.org
FreeCampsites.net

EuroCampings.co.uk
Pitchup.com
Camping.info

Work Abroad

Getting an official job abroad is often more living-focused than travel-focused (if you can really distinguish between the two), but you better believe you can get some traveling done from a cruise ship or during a stint teaching foreign language in Taiwan. It's an adventurous endeavor, but the tourist looking glass is practically non-existent when you go this route. If you dream of working and living abroad, do it. Like . . . now. It's too easy to put off, and you'll get stuck doing just that if you wait.

Most travel-related work opportunities will guide you through the process of getting hired and getting logistical ducks in a row to make things official. Programs accustomed to foreign employees often help you find room and board, or even include it in your contract! Start brainstorming your career opportunities by considering these work abroad opportunities:

Teaching

There are opportunities for nearly any subject, but the easiest option is often teaching whatever language you're fluent in. Websearch "teach [subject or language] abroad" and see where it leads you. There's also the option to teach remotely using sites like Italki.com or advertising yourself through a personal webpage.

Cruises and Seafaring

From stage performance, to kid's club leaders, to restaurant staff, and more, there are loads of opportunities on cruise ships! Our travel hacking guru Jason Moore from Chapter 5 has a great primer on his website ZerotoTravel.com called "How To Get A Job On A Cruise Ship," so start there or with a websearch of "work on a cruise ship."

Sailboats and yachts also have tons of crew options, but the work ain't easy. Both with cruises and other boats, hours tend to be long, but crew options can be especially physically taxing. Nonetheless, adventure is adventure, so websearch "crew on a boat" to begin your pirate phase!

Working Holiday Visas

These visas are granted to younger people (usually up to 30 or 35) to encourage travel while boosting employee prospects for the hosting country. Most of these opportunities are established as reciprocal agreements between countries, so your options vary depending on your passport. Find the "Working holiday visa" entry on Wikipedia.org for a breakdown of your options.

Digital Nomadism

Though it's more difficult to get an extended visa as a digital nomad, you don't always need one—just move on when your regular tourist visa runs out! Find contract work on Upwork.com, fiverr.com, TaskRabbit. com, or Outsource.com. If you don't want to bid for jobs or already have your business up and running, optimize life on the road by visiting NomadList.com and GitHub.com with the search term "awesome digital nomads."

Nannying

Being an au pair or nanny abroad is pretty self-explanatory. Options tend to be plentiful, but so does competition, so it's important that you have experience and truly love kids. Get started with (you guessed it) a websearch: "[au pair or nanny] jobs abroad."

Seasonal and Outdoor Work

Tourist hotspots and seasonal operations can more easily hire foreign workers due to the intermittent nature of employment. Sports like skiing, snowboarding, surfing, scuba diving, cycle touring, and more all look for seasonal workers doing anything from teaching, to tour guiding, to operations, to babysitting.

Here are a few places to begin your search for **seasonal work abroad**:

GoAbroad.com	Gapyear.com
Backroads.com	GoOverseas.com
SeasonWorkers.com	Trektravel.com (for cycling)

Restaurant and Service Industry Work

Restaurant chains, hotels, and resorts often have visa programs to let you hone those food service or concierge skills. Try **Jobs.GoAbroad.com** or **OneWorld365.org/jobs**. Though more touch-and-go, you can often travel somewhere and see who's hiring just by walking around and asking—especially if you have bartending skills and are in a party town. It might not be legal, though, so be careful.

Well-Being and Special Interest

If you can teach a class, course, or workshop in well-being or other special interest topics, see if there are opportunities to do so abroad. You can often stay in hotels for free in exchange for teaching a series of classes for hotel guests. Club Med is a well-known international resort that provides opportunities for nomads, but many others may do so without strongly advertising it—just shoot them an email or search online!

Peace Corps

When compared to work-exchange, the Peace Corps feels more like working abroad than free travel. Still, it may be worth considering if you want to live for free while working in a structured environment with a two-year minimum commitment.

P2P Rentals

Here's a well-kept secret: there's a free way to stay in P2P rentals like Airbnb, and sometimes even hostels. If the spot has more than one available room or is a dormitory of sorts, frequent turnaround means hosts may want a break from cleaning and changing sheets. If you can find one of these hosts (check their profile for available rentals), offer cleaning services in exchange for a free place to sleep. Give yourself some bargaining leverage and start by offering to change the sheets. If they don't bite, up the offer with more cleaning duties.

Top P2P Rental Websites:

9Flats.com	Wimdu.com
Airbnb.com	Housetrip.com
Stay22.com	VRBO.com
HomeAway.com	LoveHomeSwap.com

Pay All The Way

If you do have to pay for a bed, try to find something with a kitchen so you can at least save on meals. Here are my go-tos when paying:

Hotels:

Hotels.com
Booking.com
Expedia.com
Priceline.com
HotelsCombined.com

HotelTonight.com
Agoda.com (for Asia)
Tingo.com (careful—refunds if price drops, but non-refundable if not)

Hostels:

HostelBookers.com
HostelWorld.com
Agoda.com

Booking.com
Hostelz.com
FamousHostels.com

 ## Interlude: The Bottlenose: Up Close and Personal / Devon, England

My right hand holds a shot glass half-filled with Bailey's Irish Cream and the rest with Jameson Whiskey. The brown and beige liquors commingle as they hover over a pint filled halfway with dark, frothing Guinness Stout. I drop the shot glass.

As the three liquids merge, I rush the concoction down my throat. My third *Irish Slammer* in two hours. "Also your last," says my body … at least for tonight.

It's Mr. Jams' and my final night of a three-week pub stint in England's South West Devon coast. It's been over a year since we left America, and being here—*living* here—has felt just like that: living. It seems that the nomadic state of being has finally become second nature.

Mr. Jams stays up celebrating with our host, Henry (the pub's owner), his nephew, Little Oscar (and sole employee), and our co-volunteers, but I take my alcohol-imbued self to bed. Climbing the darkened stairs, I land on the narrow hallway connecting four rooms and the lone bathroom that six humans somehow share peacefully.

Maria's room comes first. She's a mid-40s Spaniard with an immense desire to follow rules that don't necessarily exist (while pressuring you to do the same). For the past two decades, she's lived in Madrid with her cat and parents while working as an office assistant.

When the bogeyman of Spain's 2008 economic downturn claimed her income, she took what was possibly her life's biggest departure from comfort and set off to work-exchange in the UK. The plan was to improve her English and increase prospects of returning home to a new job. As someone who doesn't enjoy peers telling me how I should do basic tasks like mopping or dishwashing, I butt heads with Maria and we try to steer clear of each other.

Next, I pass Lucine's room. Beautiful, young, and shy, French Lucine smiles constantly, but spends most of her time on Skype with her boyfriend in Paris. It is difficult to coax words from her in any language, despite her work-exchange quest to become English-proficient. The hours spent speaking French with her lover heal her *coeur nostalgique*—her homesick heart—but they do nothing for her spotty English. She works hard in the pub, though, so we don't complain.

Our bedroom lies at one end of the hall, and at the other is Henry's. He rooms with Little Oscar (who, don't worry, is 21 and actually quite tall and wide. It's his baby face that earned his nickname). The room is large, and Little Oscar finds partial privacy tucked into a corner alcove with a twin bed.

Contrary to the ruddy cheeks and sizeable presence of his young nephew, Henry is a gaunt, 40-something man with granite eyes and translucent, papery skin. His thin lips tend toward closure, but the silent lines on his face tell me more about him than conversation ever could. Another person might interpret his terse demeanor as meanness, but it's clear that there's a sensitive spirit in there somewhere.

When Little Oscar and I walk through the tide pools one day, he lets slip that Henry recently had a young wife and, more recently, a nasty divorce. I piece her together from remnants found around the house: scribbles on notebooks in forgotten drawers, group photos taped to a left-behind easel, books on meditation and healing crystals. I don't know why she left, but she did—and quickly.

Despite the weight of spoiled love, Henry is a fun and generous host. He claims that taking on this many volunteers at the same time had been a booking mistake, but I think he wanted to ensure he'd stay distracted.

Given the surplus, we each only work two to four hours during the five required work days. Two of us take the morning bathroom and restaurant cleaning duties, while the others take lunch and dinner shifts running food and washing dishes.

The schedule is easy, and whether working or not, all meals come from the delicious menu of traditional British fare. Bangers and mash (sausages and potatoes), ploughman's lunch (focaccia, chutney, cheddar or stilton, and ham), steak and fries, and enough other made-to-order options to cause a heart attack. Working in this amazing little piece of tradition, I expect my cholesterol to rise at similar rates as my contentment.

Meanwhile, we all do what we can to cheer up Henry. Mr. Jams and I have discovered one surefire way to elicit a smile: challenge him to backgammon. Henry was bullied growing up, but discovered that if he couldn't win fistfights, he could find victory in mental feats. I see bliss as his competitive streak leads him to dominate the backgammon board, and I don't mind losing so much.

As noise from the bar downstairs fades, I stumble my way toward my room through the dark hallway in the Island of Misfit Toys. The lights are still on when I climb into bed, but I'm too tired and too lazy to turn them off. I set my alarm, pull the sheets over my head, and drift into peaceful, mildly drunken sleep.

The next morning, I'm last to wake and go downstairs for breakfast. Three Slammers will do that to a person. Mr. Jams and Henry sit window-side in a wooden booth as sun filters in, lighting their backgammon game. Amidst small talk about our departure plans, our host directs a casual question to me:

"Do you remember coming into my room last night?"

Mr. Jams stares at me, grinning, and I assume they're joking. They snicker as they wait for an answer, and I finally ask Henry what he's talking about. Matter-of-factly, he says:

"You came into my room last night and did yoga."

My eyes narrow on the two grown men, now giggling with the silliness of little boys with a shared secret. I run through my memory of going to bed, setting the alarm, and waking up in the very same bed. My clothing for each event was consistent: a tank top and a trusty pair of black, sagging granny panties.

Panic rising, I repeat my question:

"What are you talking about?"

The boys share one more co-conspiring look. Then, as though telling a child why the sky is blue, Henry explains that a few minutes after he got into bed with a book, I brashly swung open his bedroom door, looked him straight in the eyes, and said:

"Oh, I'm sorry, I didn't know this was your room."

Of *course* I had known it was his room—it was one of *just four* in the pub I'd called home for the last three weeks. What was going on?

Perversely pleased at my straining smile, Henry hammers home the final details:

"Then, without a second thought, you walked across the room and stood to face the wall in front of my bed. You took a deep breath while raising your arms above your head, then bent forward—legs straight, mind you—to touch your toes. After a few moments—great form, I might add!— you calmly exited the room without another glance in my direction."

My thoughts grow fuzzy. I have no recollection of what Henry is telling me, but I see that it's the truth. I sleep-walked, yes, but I also gave Henry a zoomed-in view of my granny-pantied *derrier*. Judging from his apparent good humor, it didn't seem to bother him. Mr. Jams giggles, shrugs, and giggles some more. They get back to their game.

This, I realize, is a rare form of what it means to get up close and personal with the world while traveling. My face a shade of red common to us gingers, I go upstairs to fetch the bags. When it comes time to bid farewell to our wonderful and [very] personal new friends, I find I'm quite ready to say goodbye … and *namaste*.

Part Four: Exploring There

You've just touched down in your first city. Hurrah! Congrats! Months of planning and preparation have finally culminated in *terra nova*. But … now what? How do you hit the ground running without running into financial ruin? How do you even get out of that freakin' travel terminal?

Among all our free travel ambitions, typical sightsee tourism can be one of the most difficult to keep free. Not because it's actually difficult, but because we're trained that spending money while traveling is normal. It's one of those rules we forget we're allowed to question.

It's not that I think you should skip paying for sites that are truly amazing and cost money. It's just that I think you should choose wisely. You can truly come to know a place without spending a dime, but sometimes that dime is worth it.

The following chapters will help you discern the truth in a way that's cost free at best and cost-effective at worst. Throw on those socks with sandals and let's hit the road!

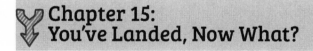

Chapter 15: You've Landed, Now What?

Foreign language! Money exchange! Hawkers selling wares and taxi drivers pushing rides! No doubt, stepping into a bustling travel terminal can be disorienting. Here are **five money-saving touchdown essentials** to send you on your worry-free way.

1. Pack Food

Terminal food is dull, overpriced, and kinda yucky. And nearby fast food will only shrink finances and expand fat cells. Pack your own road snacks instead. Never go hungry, and save your hard-earned money for a delicious and memorable local dining experience instead.

2. Be Language-Aware

Call me old-fashioned, but I encourage you not to rely on a tech device for translation. Buy and always carry a phrasebook and study it before departure. If nothing else, learn basic niceties, greetings, and farewells, like *Please, Thank you, Excuse me, Do you speak English?, I'm sorry I don't speak [foreign language]*, and *Can you help me please?* I can't emphasize enough how much this will improve your experience and help locals warm up to you.

Adapting to a new culture is difficult and humbling, but that's one of its greatest rewards! Approach all situations with a smile and the willingness to laugh at yourself if you mess up a translation. Lord knows the locals will be laughing at you—might as well join them. This will put people at ease, and they'll be more likely to attempt to decipher the gibberish coming out of your mouth.

 TALES FROM THE ROAD: People say the French are notorious for their snooty reception of foreigners, but I've found the stereotype grossly overstated. Why? Because I've always attempted to speak French before defaulting to English, even if it meant literally making up words and adding a little *je ne sais quoi* for some flair. It was comically embarrassing, and it totally worked! Because I made small, sincere attempts to show respect for their language, French locals received me with compassion and camaraderie. And a little laughter.

3. Keep Relevant Phone Numbers and Addresses Nearby

Wherever you're headed, keep multiple copies of all necessary and important contact information for that destination saved in multiple locations. And not just on your phone! You never know when that battery will die and you're nowhere near a power source.

4. Know Where You Are

Travel hubs are often located near tourism hot spots, so consider taking advantage of geography and catching any must-sees on your way to other destinations. Travel is an exercise in living without regrets; as wallet-friendly as it is to rush from one free accommodation to another, take advantage of once-in-a-lifetime opportunities to explore local points of interest—yes, even if they cost money. You'll live with regret (*gasp!*) if you end a trip realizing you were within two hours of Istanbul and its renowned Hagia Sophia or the famous spice bazaar and you (*gasp!*) missed it.

5. Have an Exit Plan

Research transportation options for getting out of your touchdown location *before* you arrive. Terminal employees might be able to help, but they won't know all the free or least-expensive routes. Oftentimes, they'll only know the most popular and expensive options since those are the ones being marketed.

This could be a great place to launch your hitchhiking moxy! If that doesn't work, arrival terminals are still prime places to catch a bus, train, or rideshare.

 PRO TIP: Shuttles and buses are far cheaper than taxis. The caveat is that some only operate at certain times and days of the week. Search online for terms like "cheapest way to get to [your destination] from [travel hub]" or "airport express to/from [your destination]," translating when necessary.

Chapter 16: The Savvy Tourist

Oh, the ways to see a city for free! This is where many travelers flounder, spending in a few days what could have supported them for *months* of additional travel. We've covered how life abroad can be completely free, but if you want to weave a few paid experiences into your journey, it shouldn't compromise the rest of your travels. Weave away (the modern nomad way)!

Many vacationers like to adopt a *laissez-faire* money-spending attitude once their feet hit the road. Cares and worries from back home tend to fade away. This is a beautiful side-effect of travel, but it can also be a trap. Keep an eye on your cash so that all those wonderful memories aren't marred by a multi-page bank statement.

TALES FROM THE ROAD: It's 100% possible to spend a week in Paris for under $84—I've done it. I had an *amazing* time, too. Want to know how?

Accommodation: I housesat for a friend of a friend (*vive les relations!*) and left a "thank you!" bottle of wine.

Cost: $8

Meals: One "fancy" French dinner ($30), one delicious authentic meal in Chinatown ($16), groceries ($30).

Cost: $76

Tourism: I visited museum highlights on free days and otherwise explored cultural gems like flea markets, parks, and other renowned spots.

Cost: $0

Transportation: I walked everywhere, which was a great excuse to not do other exercise stuff!

Cost: $0

Going with the flow is what the cool kids do—I get it. But if you want to go with the flow for as long as possible, do it without throwing money away. The cool kids don't have to know that you did a little advanced planning in order to get that flow on.

I've said it before—think of time spent researching and planning as *paid* time. All the money you will save is payment for the hours you logged. The following sections will provide a better understanding of this mentality, and you'll be introduced to some of the many deals that will turn you into a free-ish tourist extraordinaire.

Ground Rules of the Savvy Spender

1. Minimize Trips to the ATM

Look into the terms of your bank's debit or credit cards. Most banks charge withdrawal fees on *top* of the fee charged by using an ATM outside your banking network, especially if it's in a foreign country. It's best to withdraw as much as you feel comfortable having in your wallet at one time. However, a good safety tip is dividing up your cash and keeping it in different spots, like a wallet, your daypack, boot, or socks. Alternately, you may be able to find bank cards with strong overseas networks or reimbursements for overseas banking fees.

2. Create a Budget and Track Spending

Apps like **Expensify, Mint**, and **PocketGuard** will keep you from having to go home early due to lack of funds. Or just keep a detailed, handwritten record. This makes your spending concrete and accessible, enabling you to make real-time decisions on whether or not that late-night foam party in Madrid is worth it.

3. Avoid Foreign Transaction Fees

You've learned about travel hacking, so by now you should be working toward a fruitful travel rewards card with minimal or nonexistent foreign transaction fees.

 KEEP YO' MONEY: The right credit or debit card depends on individual travel needs; Chase Sapphire, Charles Schwab Debit, and Cash Passport are great starting points to investigate!

4. Don't Exchange with Street Hawkers

You're just inviting a scam. Go to an accredited bank or reliable currency exchange store. Never exchange cash in an airport—the fees are always higher!

 TECH TIP: Download **XE Currency** App to convert currency using rates that update whenever the app is online.

5. Use Local Currency

Even if dollars from home are welcome, they usually make a profit on the exchange rate. That being said, it's always helpful to pack USD 100 to 200 in case of emergency.

6. Know the Conversion Rate

Things don't have to be exact every time (usually they won't be). Just make sure you're not getting taken advantage of with a particularly crazy rate, and always count your money before leaving the currency exchange desk.

Sights on a Shoestring

Keep your budget secure once you hit the streets. Here's how:

Maximize Discounts

If you already know the museums, monuments, or other attractions you'd like to visit, research their free or reduced admission days and adjust your plans accordingly. Check websites like Groupon or LivingSocial. Membership cards like AAA or a student ID will score you discounts, too (I might be guilty of using a 10-year-old student ID card ... *might* be). And finally, whether you're travelling alone or with a group, it never hurts to politely ask for a discount. You may be pleasantly surprised.

INSIDER INFO: Know when tourist attractions are closed! Many European businesses and attractions close on Sunday and/or Monday. Put destination holy days and holidays in your calendar to know when not to show up.

Tourist Passes

Tourist passes are often overlooked, but they can be your golden ticket to a quick way of seeing as many popular sights as possible. With a one-time purchase, you gain access to museums and other attractions plus discounts on transportation, restaurants, and bars. Inspect the fine print to know which hours and days are available to use the pass—it usually comes with restrictions!

Read reviews of the places included with the pass to make sure it's worth your time and money. If you prefer a more intimate, original, or slower-paced tourist experience, passes may not be for you. But if you were already planning to purchase individual tickets to these activities, go for it!

P2P Sharing Economy Tourism

The number of websites and apps that connect travelers with locals for unique experiences keeps growing. Both paid and free options provide traditional sightseeing or behind-the-scenes looks at a city's culture and community. Find secret jazz spots, the best indie movie theaters, a local's favorite biking route, or dinner with a group of old friends.

Check out **these sites to experience the city like a local**:

YowTrip.com

Meetup.com

Vayable.com

WithLocals.com

PartyWith.co

AirBnB Experiences

GetYourGuide.com

Covering Ground

Look Down

There is an oft-overlooked free mode of transportation at your constant disposal—your feet! If you tend to *forget* your exercise routine when traveling, walking is an excellent substitution. Studies have shown that walking the same distance as a jogging route provides similar health benefits, so why not?[4]

If our hunter-gatherer ancestors could cover 10 to 12 miles in a day just to eat, is it so outlandish to believe that we can do the same just to catch a new gallery exhibit? Our bodies haven't changed *that* much! Scientists actually attribute most of today's common ailments—diabetes, cardiovascular disease, and cancer—to our newfound love of sedentary living.[5] Killin' it!

Start early, take lots of sightseeing breaks, wear comfortable shoes, and pack snacks and water. Walking gives you a ground level, intimate understanding of a city that you just can't get any other way.

 **INSIDER INFO:** Many cities offer websites and meetups pointing you to free walking tours. Web-search "free walking tour [city name]" to find one.

If you're paying for accommodation, this is the time to spend a bit more on a centrally located room since you'll be able to save on transportation costs. It's also easier to break up the mileage by using your digs as a rest or meal stop before heading in a new direction. Walking a mile only takes about 15 minutes. In a busy city, that beats a taxi ride *and* you don't have to deal with road rage!

Deals on Wheels

Yet another healthy and inexpensive way to cover ground is with rental bicycles and electric scooters. Rent from a brick-and-mortar store, a street-level kiosk, or locals using sites like Craigslist.com. Many rentals allow you to rent at one side of the city and return at another. Some have specific pickup and drop-off points, and others are connected to

---

[4] https://www.prevention.com/fitness/a20477492/how-walking-is-healthier-than-running/

[5] https://www.ncbi.nlm.nih.gov/pmc/articles/PMC3404815/

an app with a locking system that enables you to rent and return almost anywhere.

Sign-up terms vary per country—some use apps or a regular credit card, while others require purchasing an activation number in a store. Often the first 30 minutes are free, which means you can rent, return, and re-rent throughout the day without spending a dime. Be careful to read the fine print—these systems can be notoriously confusing, especially in a foreign language!

KEEP YO' MONEY: Ask to borrow a bike on local community message boards or groups, like those found on Craigslist.com, Couchsurfing.com, or Facebook. Offer to trade for a pack of beer or delicious dinner and promise to return it in good condition. Sometimes offering a collateral item like a cash deposit helps.

Going Public

When walking or biking doesn't do the trick, opt for public transportation. Like walking, there's a particular sense of victory getting to know and then successfully navigating a city by riding the bus with locals. Familiarize yourself with ticketing systems in advance and be open to getting help from strangers, if only to avoid being that person holding up the line because you can't understand the instructions on the ticket kiosk screen.

If you've done your research ahead of time (because you're a savvy traveler who reads amazing travel books!), you (1) won't overspend on unnecessary tickets, (2) have the correct amount of money at the ready, and (3) made your purchase like a (local) boss!

Taxis are to be avoided! They cost way too much. Find a popular local rideshare app—Lyft and Uber probably aren't the only players in whatever town you're in. If you're a first-time rider, search for special coupons and deals—many first rides are discounted or free!

Boost the Odds: Bonus Tips and Reminders

Several other apps will enhance your visit, but as we know, apps enter and leave the market faster than Hogwarts goes through Defence Against the Dark Arts professors. Book jokes! In addition to the ones listed below, find the most recent and relevant options with an online search. Download these apps before arriving at your destination while you have a Wi-Fi connection to ensure you get what you want out of a place. Many will work without data connectivity, so consider offline options based on your data plan.

Maps and Tourism Apps:

Google Maps, HERE WeGo, or Maps.me - You can use these without any network connection for maps (good guess!), points of interest, and directions.

Citymapper - Optimized transportation routes with real-time updates
Fon Wi-Fi Finder - Hot dog! This shows areas that offer free Wi-Fi.

AroundMe, Sygic Travel, or Triposo - These apps are informative travel guides that use GPS to show you nearby theatres, cafes, bus stations, and other goodies and can work offline.

Google Translate - Make sure you download your language of interest for offline translation!

Random Goodies

Yayyy! We live in a world where investing in each other and building a sharing community among strangers is seen as fun! Unless you're kind of terrible! Here are a few **more peer-sharing websites** to whet your appetite for travel:

Ridehunting.com - rent bikes, skis, or snowboards from a local
Coworking.org - find shareable workspace abroad
Meet2Talk.com - language-learning platform for practicing face-to-face

If none of those work, find city message boards on Facebook and Couchsurfing.com. Search "[city name] locals" and see what comes up. If you write a post in the local language, people will often jump at the chance to help you think of fun, free, or off the beaten path activities. Get creative, have fun, and take that free travel mojo wherever you go!

Roughly 80% of the reason I travel is to discover and eat delicious food. It's a lovely addictive habit in which we're *encouraged* to indulge. In fact, we'd die if we didn't—so there. My favorite habit is saving your life!

Great food experiences are integral to amazing travel (I state that as fact, not opinion); it follows that if such experiences are free, then your budget is made available for other things. Just like vacationers who dole out big money for fancy dining, free travelers can have equally memorable dining experiences *without* breaking the bank.

I've had duck confit shepherd's pie in the French countryside. I've helped prepare locally-hunted wild boar ragu in Tuscany. I've folded miniature raviolis alongside freakishly energetic Turkish women by the Black Sea. I've scooped the "meat" out of freshly grilled eggplant on an Israeli beach for *baba ganoush*. These are just a few of the amazing tastes that stand out to me from my travels, and none of them occurred in a restaurant or required a single euro, lira, or shekel.

Remember all of those less-than-memorable (or memorable for the wrong reasons) meals you've had while traveling? A bland pasta dish on a crowded city square, a soggy plastic-wrapped sandwich from a tourist attraction food stall, or a hardened croissant in a street-side cafe? Those are all easy and cheap to make, but you probably paid a premium instead. Silly traveler!

Restaurants aren't a waste of money by definition, but you need to consider the trade-offs. If you save $5 to $20 each day by resisting that dine-out breakfast or lunch, after a few days you'll have enough for a truly amazing—maybe even expensive—meal. Think about opportunity cost: $20 per day on dining out equates to $140 a week. What else could you have done with $140? It's enough for a flight, a night or two in a snazzy hotel, or 47 artisan chocolate bars.

A note on restaurants: We're not banning them completely. What we're aiming for is to maximize eating experiences (restaurant-inclusive) without missing out on other amazing travel experiences.

Along with free accommodation-provided meals, there are three main other options for feeding yourself for free or cheap while traveling: (1)

preparing food for yourself, (2) dumpster diving, or (3) dining out. Some are free, but for the ones that aren't, we're going to do it right.

Let's dig in, shall we? *Bon appetit!*

 ## Interlude: Dining Disasters / East Ireland

My first sighting of Margaret will be forever etched in my memory.

After a successful start as a pastry chef in Dublin, Margaret was soon tired of city life and longed for a calmer, quiet existence in the country. Newly married, she sold husband Dan (whom you met in an earlier interlude) on her plan to use her business earnings to buy a big home in the countryside. He reluctantly agreed.

They splurged on renovations, and when finally complete, their new country home featured six huge bedrooms, three bathrooms, a high-ceilinged cafe-sized kitchen, two sitting rooms, panoramic windows exposing endless landscape views, and a renovated barn just across the driveway that served as Margaret's new bakery.

She specialized in British treats like handmade pies, tarts, quiches, relishes, chutneys, and jams. The pastry crusts were golden and flakey, the fillings moist and savory, and nearly all of this was proudly made from scratch.

Margaret and Dan's initial plan was to open a small cafe in town where Margaret could sell her delectable treats along with coffee and tea. For additional income, Dan would make weekly two-hour round-trip deliveries to cafes and restaurants in Dublin and surrounding towns.

In 2007, not long into their plan, the bottom fell out of Ireland's economy. Just like that, Margaret and Dan became owners of an enormous mortgage and a business model they simply couldn't support. With two young children to raise, they couldn't afford to move back to Dublin, so they devised a survival plan centered around work-exchange.

Hoping that customs officials wouldn't notice and that neighbors would keep mum, work-exchangers arrived from all over the world to serve as cafe and bakery staff or to help with home upkeep. It was quite probably illegal, but for the foreign workers it was a treat. For Margaret, Dan, and the kids, it was their lifeboat—a saving grace.

The home, which was spacious and cozy before work-ex-change life, soon bustled with new faces. By the time I arrived, work-exchangers had been popping in and out for close to six years. Apart from general bakery duties, many workers turned into part-time nannies: for the chil-dren, Frankie and Dot, an influx of volunteers was simply par for the course—a familiar lifestyle since the ages of five and seven.

When I arrive, Dan retrieves me from the train station, we get to the house and he leads me into the barn-cum-com-mercial bakery. My eyes widen at the heavenly world in-side: in the first room, a quadruple-sized industrial oven holds court while two 20-somethings stamp out pastry toppers for miniature meat pies.

Crossing into a larger main kitchen, we spot three other busy volunteers. Amid the whirring appliances, a mid-dle-aged Asian woman smiles at us briefly before returning to a red stand mixer filled with whipping cream. A brunette in her 30s stands beside another steaming oven, waiting to check a batch of delicate meringues. Guarding the dish-washing station is a bespectacled boy no older than 18.

On the other side of the room, about 40 feet away, with her back to us, Margaret spreads out the batter for what I would come to learn is her famous whiskey cake. Because my shoes aren't close-toed as safety standards require, we stay put while Dan attempts to get his wife's attention. After the fourth try, the spatula freezes, she lifts her head, and her pale face abruptly turns to face us.

I'm overtaken by a pang of surprise—her eyes are encir-cled by the shadows of many sleepless nights; they con-trast sharply with wisps of bright red hair escaping from beneath her black baker's cap. There's no kind description for what I see in Margaret at that moment: a fairytale witch, broken broom in hand, desperately trying to find her way after crash-landing. I'm mesmerized.

Her mouth hangs open as she stares at us, trying to switch her focus from the batter to why her Dan stands there with an unfamiliar grinning woman. Snapping-to, she remembers her life and how new faces constantly appear throughout. She quickly flashes a smile and a hello in my direction before turning back to the cake.

Something about it leaves me dazed as Dan leads me out of the kitchen and across the gravel driveway to the main house. An Irish setter wags his body in excitement and follows as Dan takes me to my room and recommends I spend the day relaxing. With that, he rushes off in the van for another of many errands.

It takes me a few hours to realize that although it had not been mentioned in their profile or our correspondence, up to eight volunteers are concurrently staying in this home built for four. Since Mr. Jams would be joining me in about a week, we're lucky to snag a large bedroom with a reading nook looking out over the rolling hills. It's perfectly situated for sunsets.

Many of the other volunteers were also unaware that they would have co-work-exchangers. Over my stay, I watch several hide their surprise upon realizing they'll be sharing a room with a stranger.

Later that evening, I hear Margaret rummaging in the kitchen, so I go downstairs to let her know that I've recently gone gluten free. Their host profile states explicitly that they don't accommodate special diets, but I'm somehow convinced I can avoid the gluten without causing her extra work.

My plan is to assure her I don't expect any special meal adjustments for me. If the dish is pasta, for example, I'll simply eat the sauce and any side dishes. If that doesn't work, I'll happily eat food that I've brought with me.

As it turns out, I'm being optimistic … not realistic.

I walk into the vast kitchen as Margaret shuffles back and forth with the same haste and fervor I'd seen earlier in the barn bakery. I call out her name a couple of times from the doorway. No response. *Déjà vu.*

I try one more time and she jerks around with steamed cheeks and a familiar startled expression. I attempt to remind her of our earlier meeting that day and after a quick "hello," she patiently informs me that she's "kind of busy." Like an employer who's had to say this a million times before me, she turns back to the food.

For better or worse, I continue:

"I just wanted to say … by no means do I want to create extra work for you, but if you could just set things aside if it was a question of mixing gluten foods in with non-gluten, that'd be great. I mean it's not a big deal but I'm just trying—if it's okay—not to eat gluten and—"

But before I drone on about how I don't want to make things difficult, she cuts me off—

"I don't do anything for special diets."

My face flushes and turns a red only redheads can understand. But Margaret doesn't notice because, without missing a beat, she's already turned back to her boiling water.

"Oh," I realize, "we're having pasta."

Sputtering an, "Okay, thanks" I back out of the kitchen and go upstairs to hide. Trying to process the perceived cold-bloodedness of this woman has my nerves rattling. In all the hosts I've encountered who were rude to each *other*, I'd never had one speak to *me* so curtly, especially so early on.

I try to ignore my glaring misstep. I know. I *did* read that they don't adjust meals. But their setup—their facility, if I can call it that—was so attractive for this food-lover that I'd chosen to keep mum about my gluten-free diet until I'd snagged the gig. It wasn't my best or most honest decision.

The kids call us down for dinner after 20 useless minutes of fretting, and I file out of my room to join seven other volunteers in the kitchen. Seeing the smiling faces of my co-volunteers, I try to follow suit.

The next morning, as with most of them, Margaret will be up at 4 a.m. to start all over again. Rinse, wash, repeat, so to speak. She's in a constant state of survival mode, fighting to maintain a lifestyle she chose for her family— the same lifestyle that put them in the financial red-zone.

At dinner, the moment when the 12 of us sit down and only have to work on eating, Margaret smiles effortlessly. It's a rare work-free moment in her life. I realize that Margaret—day after endless day—is exhausted. And suddenly? Forgivable. I dish up on pasta and forget about our earlier exchange.

By the end of my three weeks there, I have eaten *very* well. Contrary to her seemingly staunch stance, Margaret makes amendments for my diet, ensuring there's always something gluten-free for me to fill up on, even though she doesn't and shouldn't have to.

And I'll tell you this: it was always delicious.

Chapter 17: Practical Provisions

We often purchase subpar meals simply because meal prep on the road isn't the norm. But why spend money on food that *isn't* special when it can instead be used to create an experience you'll treasure forever? If you seek longevity, excitement, and variety in your travels, make your own menu instead of ordering from one.

The Accommodation Relation

Travelers usually dine out to experience different food cultures, but restaurants rarely reach the level of authenticity you can get sitting in a local's kitchen. These days, it's easy—just eat up those delectable food memories during work-exchange! Find the hosts with positive cooking reviews or who mention their love of good food in their profile (if you skipped Chapter 11 but like this idea, now would be the time to go check it out).

Free meals often make appearances with couchstays and housesitting gigs, but they're not guaranteed like on a work-exchange where getting fed is usually part of the program. When housesitting, homeowners may leave you with a stocked kitchen and grant you free reign (if this isn't explicitly stated, you can request it as one of the terms of your housesit arrangement). Couchstay hosts might cook you a meal out of the goodness of their heart, but helping yourself to the kitchen is a no-no unless it's been offered.

As far as paid accommodations go, don't save on a cheap bed then spend your savings on food. Find places with kitchen access and a refrigerator so you can prepare and store food. If breakfast is included with your rate, don't skip it, but don't fill up on sugars and cheap processed food either (which often play starring roles at free breakfast events)! Find hearty, protein-rich food and take fruit to-go whenever possible.

At hotel check-ins, turn up your charm and request a room upgrade—sometimes they'll throw in a free breakfast or room with a kitchenette or mini fridge. Many provide free snacks at the check-in desk, spa, or lobby such as fruit or mixed nuts. Don't be shy. Take some whenever you pass—that's why it's there.

Preparing Food for Yourself

Do you think it's better to have one amazing meal in 10 cities or 10 amazing meals in one city? If you want a bigger variety of experiences overall, allocate funds so that meals aren't where you spend the most money while traveling. Yes, having culturally compelling food is important, but it should be balanced with your desire to see and do lots of new and interesting things. Barring any fast food restaurants (yuck!) or known inexpensive countries, the cheapest way to do this is often by preparing your own food.

Remember that stall hawking $9 sandwiches to clueless tourists? How about a loaf of whole grain bread, sliced cheddar, deli salami, and a few pocketed packets of mustard and mayo? Suddenly, $9 equals sandwiches for a week! Even if you're kitchen-averse, there are plenty of simple and labor-free options like the aforementioned sandwich hack.

When it comes to concocting your own meals, avoid cheap items that will only cause you to spend *more* in the long run. If it's not filling and nutritious at the outset, you'll be hungry again in an hour and just have to buy more stuff. Skip the Wonder Bread and Nutella and opt for bulgur (just add water!), a tin

 DO THE MATH: Find the per-weight cost by dividing an item's price by its weight. A snack-size 1.5-ounce bag of chips costs $0.99 and a normal 8.5-ounce bag costs $2.99. So, the small size is $0.66 per ounce, and the large is $0.35 per ounce. That means the small is nearly *double* the price of the large.

of smoked mackerel (tastes like tuna, but the fish is less endangered), and some easy-eating vegetables like carrots and lettuce.

Educate yourself on nutritional information in order to know the food's value and "fill" factor. A bag of chips is cheap, but the lack of nutrition makes it pointless. Mixed nuts or granola are better buys; they cost more, but you'll eat less and stay full longer with the added protein. That means less spending overall. Similarly, avoid bread-heavy meals like bagels, sandwiches with meager fillings, two-bite pastries, etc.— empty calories, empty carbs … empty wallet.

The Gear

If you want to be a vagabond food *artiste*, there are a **few minor tools** you might want to carry.

- ⇨ Utensil set - Plasticware is wasteful, so sharpen your reusable spork or practice your chopstick skills. The **Joseph GoEat Compact Stainless-Steel Cutlery Set** or the **Light My Fire Spoon-Fork-Knife Combo** are great options.

- ⇨ Collapsible food storage - Containers like these **Thin Bins** are your three-in-one mixing bowl, storage container, and "plate" on-the-go. **Reusable silicone food storage bags** might also be helpful.

⇨ Pocket Multitool - There's no telling the ways this will come in handy. Rest assured, it will. I like the **Victorinox Swiss Army Minichamp**, but remember they aren't allowed in your carry-on bag when going through airport security.

An Idea Worth *Retaining*

Packing your own food storage containers will seem excessive to the minimalist traveler, but it is *so* not. God bless those strange Tupperware parties that zig-zagged across 20th century American living rooms; they're probably why America is one of the few countries that doesn't regard a doggy bag and eating leftovers as bizarre.

When housesitting for a man just outside of Rome, he made a pizza for my arrival. It was *de-li-cious*. The freshly sliced mozzarella and *parmigiano reggiano* oozed off crisp homemade crust. I ate until I could eat no more—but there *was* more. I put the remaining slice on a plate (there was no Tupperware) and went to place it in the fridge, but he quickly held up his hand and motioned me to leave it on the table. Assuming he would eat it later, I washed up and went to bed.

The next morning, to my horror, the once-glorious pizza slice was still on the table. Did my host not realize leftover pizza is a cross-cultural delicacy? Isn't that why microwaves were invented?! Sad, cold, and awkward, it remained there throughout the next dinner.

On the second morning, I placed a cautious footstep onto the kitchen linoleum and, searching the table, did not see the hallowed slice. Terror filling my limbs, I took two leaden steps toward the trash can, flipped back the lid with a false-casual push, and saw it lying there. Closing my eyes tight, I whispered a small prayer for forgiveness from the pizza gods.

In Greece, housesitting hosts treated Mr. Jams and me to a smorgasbord of Greek food: local lamb sausage, noodles, *spanakopita*, and much more. Our best efforts were no match—leftovers for at *least* two other dinners remained.

Using the universal sign language of *clam hands*, I asked the waiter for a to-go box. He tilted his head and looked disapprovingly at our hosts. Their eyes were lowered ... possibly in shame, but he returned with a to-go box as though holding an ancient relict. I left with the food. Victory: Meggan!

Global food waste has reached horrifying numbers—the Food and Agriculture Organization of the United Nations estimates that one-third of the world's edible food is wasted every year.[6] That's over one billion tonnes—embarrassing, right?

If food is good, if you've paid for it, and if it will keep, for the love of all things holy and delicious, take it home! Over time, this can literally save you hundreds of dollars on meals you didn't have to buy.

If you feel like a foreign weirdo asking for a doggy bag (*Sac chien*? *Bolsa de perro*? *Pes taška*? *Saco de cachorro*?), don't ask. Bring your own reusable container. It may sound even stranger, but who cares about being judged? It will get easier (I promise) and when you're grubbing for free the next day, you won't feel so bad. Neither will your belly!

Your own reusable to-go container doesn't just save food and money, it reduces waste overall. Plastic and Styrofoam never biodegrade, they just break down into smaller pieces. We're stuck with them as long as the earth spins (*Sorry, grandchildren!*). When future geologists excavate ground samples of earth, it will have a thick layer of Styrofoam restaurant to-go containers!

Store Foraging

Here are several quick, easy, and **filling meal options** found in nearly any store. Disclaimer: I'm not a food scientist, so take my recommendations on shelf life and nutrition as educated advice, not food-science fact:

⇨ Yogurt (can go at least a day without refrigeration) + jam/berries/granola

⇨ Sandwich or wrap options
  - Crackers, rice cakes, whole grain sandwich bread, wraps, cabbage leaves

⇨ Cold cut deli meats and cheeses (often half the price of pre-pack-aged slices)

⇨ Canned fish (recycle!)
  - With lemon juice, mayo, mustard, salt, and pepper packets, you can make a salad to eat with raw vegetables or on a sandwich.
  - Find tins that don't require a can opener.
  - Choose sustainable fish—you're traveling for free, but don't be a cheapskate.

---

[6] http://www.fao.org/save-food/resources/keyfindings/en/

⇨ Granola or trail mix
- Packaged cereals have more sugar and less nutrition, and won't be as filling or inexpensive as combining your own oats, nuts, and dried fruit.

⇨ Nutrition bars
- Not as cost-effective or nutritious as trail mix or granola, but low-sugar, high-protein options will help keep you full.

⇨ Cheese
- Aged cheeses like *parmigiano* and three-year-old (or older) gouda last indefinitely without refrigeration.

⇨ Cured meats
- Uncut, they require no refrigeration. Once you cut a slice, they should be eaten within a day or two without refrigeration.

⇨ Oats
- The thinner the oat, the faster it will soften with water.
- Pre-packaged oatmeal won't fill you up and is packed with sugar. Use bulk oats and add flavorings like cinnamon, honey, and raisins.
- Ask a cafe to add boiling water to the oats you've brought in with you.
- Soak oats overnight in any temperature water and they should be ready in 6-8 hours.

⇨ Fruit
- Choose hardy fruits that won't bruise if you stuff them into bags.

⇨ Nut butter (almond, cashew, etc.)
- Store-bought nut butters are expensive, so make your own. Usually they're less oily, so they can be carried in a ziplock bag for easier packing.

⇨ Peanut butter
- Although less nutritious than other nut butters, it's cheap and high in protein and fat

⇨ Jelly or jam
- Typically doesn't need refrigeration due to high sugar content
- Aim for brands with fruit as the first ingredient, not sugar

⇨ Salad greens
- A strange but surprisingly tasty snack is simply reaching into a bag of mixed greens as if they were potato chips. I was a doubter too—before I tried it. It's my go-to method for vegetables while traveling.

- ⊜ Create a salad in your to-go container by adding other ingredients. You just made a salad!
- ⊜ Add to sandwiches or eat mouthfuls along with anything that needs a fresh crunch.

⇨ Raw Vegetables
- ⊜ Cucumber, celery, carrots, tomatoes, bell peppers, radishes, broccoli florets, cabbage, and many more can all be easily eaten raw with a little salt.

⇨ Bulgur
- ⊜ This dried cracked wheat is highly nutritious and prepared simply by soaking in water.

⇨ Small jar/bottle of mixed oil and vinegar
- ⊜ Mix this yourself ahead of time after buying a small *leak-proof* bottle.
- ⊜ Great with vegetables, sandwiches, and salads.

⇨ Mixed nuts
- ⊜ The least nutritious are cashews and peanuts.

⇨ Dried fruit
- ⊜ High calorie and sugar option, so best eaten in moderation.

KEEP YO' MONEY: Make a meal out of farmer's market samples! Plus, if you visit the market closer to closing time, you can snag price-reduced food or try your hand at haggling.

If you have an irrational fear of preparing your own food, buy premade bulk items from a local deli or grocery counter whenever possible. I'm referring to items that are priced according to individual weight; these tend to be more economical than branded, pre-packaged items on store shelves.

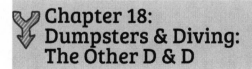

Chapter 18:
Dumpsters & Diving:
The Other D & D

I know. People throw *trash* in dumpsters! Trash is there! How can you eat something if it comes from where trash was?!

I used to work in a food store. They tossed completely edible stuff all the time. I would promptly gather the goods from the dumpster, box them up, and place them in the walk-in cooler to bring home with me later. Then I would wash my hands and get back to work.

Food rules are weird. Utterly usable grub gets tossed if (1) it looks ugly or unnatural (that orange is oval-shaped—the *horror*!), (2) it's past the best-by or sell-by date, or (3) the store simply needs to make room for other inventory.

Stuff also gets tossed if it's sincerely unusable—rotten, fermenting, etc. Dumpster diving, then, is walking the line of edible on one side, sincerely inedible on the other. It's that simple.

RETHINK IT: Expiration, best-by, use-by, and sell-by dates are much less relevant than we think. Unless it's infant formula, food companies aren't even required by law to print these dates on their products, so ultimately, they're just suggestions (mostly to help sellers keep track of things). The truth is that the date is mostly just an arbitrary number. When it comes down to it, just use your best judgment. The **USDA** agrees:

"The quality of perishable products may deteriorate after the date passes, however, such products should still be safe if handled properly. Consumers must evaluate the quality of the product prior to its consumption to determine if the product shows signs of spoilage."[7]

Here's the thing: Before you ate that carrot, it was covered in dirt and probably poop. At least a little bit of poop. Then it got cleaned, you peeled, then ate it. Before you ate that steak, it was covered in living cow and blood and stuff. It was also hanging out with poop. Because organs.

So, you pull a package of completely sealed potato chips out of a dumpster. You wash the package off with soap and water. You then wash your hands. You open the package—the contents of which have never touched outside air, let alone the trash that was briefly near it.

Is it really so bad? Come on, I know you've done grosser things than *that*.

I debated putting a dumpster diving section in this book because, let's face it, many of you are turned off by the idea. But that's exactly *why* I'm putting it in this book—the reasons to try it far outweigh the reasons not to, and it's time to shift perspective. The common sense of packaged food or cleanable fruits and veggies being edible is just too obvious for a free traveler to ignore.

---

[7] https://www.fsis.usda.gov/wps/portal/fsis/topics/food-safety-education/get-answers/food-safety-fact-sheets/food-labeling/food-product-dating/food-product-dating

There's also this: dumpster diving doesn't just have to be about *you* feeding yourself for free. It can be about feeding others. As Rob Greenfield says (he's not *just* a cycle tourist extraordinaire!) in his article **"10 Tips for Dumpster Diving Success!"**: "Flip the stigma by becoming a food waste warrior and collect food to help others out." Forget fearing that you'll look homeless when you dumpster dive—dumpster dive to *help* the homeless!

If the United Nations estimates that one-third of the world's food is wasted every year (and it does), and if we consider those who struggle to get food on the table every night (and we do), can we see that dumpster diving isn't just a means for free food, it's a means for a better planet? *We can! We can see it*!

It may just be the semantics of the term "dumpster diving" that implies something horrendous and filthy. As though inherent in the idea of dumpster diving is the promise that you will have to throw on a swimsuit and literally dive into a pool of gently lapping trash.

This isn't a requirement. You can just take a glance. You can just see, maybe, if there happens to be some pre-packaged and shelf-stable food just sitting there on the surface.

Or, you can have a dumpster diving outfit that you simply wash when you get home. This outfit might also have fashionable accessories: latex gloves, a box or crate to stand on (for when you do decide to make that entrance), a towel, some soapy water, maybe even a post-dive *second* outfit.

You got this, Sporto.

The Rules of D & D

Before you go slipping into that trash swimsuit, know that rifling through someone else's dumping grounds can be illegal. As with most things in life, using your smarts will be necessary. And as with most things in this book, I'm going to make sure you put that smart cap on correctly.

1. Know your surroundings *and* your rights

Your new planet-helping, belly-filling, trash-loving efforts might require a little trial and error. Every location will have different rules. Actually, some won't have rules at all, they'll just have people with opinions that they *think* are rules. While dumpster diving isn't explicitly illegal in most places, trespassing certainly can be. Look for signs, don't break locks, and be careful.

If an employee or security guard wants to get rough with you, it's best to know your rights. What can they respond when you tell them that dumpster diving is legal in that county and that there are zero "no trespassing" signs on the premises? Bonus points if you inform them nicely and gain respect in the process (which is what you should try for either way). Very rarely will anyone actually press charges or even have the right to do so.

> **INSIDER INFO:** When dumpsters are housed in cage or fence-like structures, this is usually either for aesthetic reasons or to dissuade outsiders from dumping trash inside. "No Dumping" does not mean the same thing as "No Taking." In fact, since most stores pay trash disposal services based on the weight of whatever's in their dumpster, they often happily turn a blind eye to divers who lighten the load. Of course, if there's a lock, this means stay out.

2. Look before you leap

Truth: There are reasons *not* to dumpster dive. Rodents, glass, bacteria-crawling food. Yuck! I don't wish that upon you; I wish you all things that are good (and tasty). The good clean truth? Retail stores tend to have their trash picked up frequently. Stuff hasn't typically been out there for long, which means less festering and whatnot.

All the same, drape a towel over the edge of the dumpster (to keep your shirt clean—what were you, raised in a barn!?) and peer in with a cautious eye to gauge whether you should hop in. Maybe even have a special dumpster diving prodding tool (stick, shovel, banana, etc.).

3. Go prepared

Ever think you'd be considering a **packing list** for a dumpster vacay? Here we go!

⇨ Protective gloves
⇨ Close-toed shoes or sturdy boots
⇨ Flashlight or headlamp
⇨ Bags, boxes, or coolers for your winnings
⇨ Post-dive change of clothes
⇨ Bottle of soapy water or hand sanitizer

⇨ Towel (unexpected wetness will happen)

⇨ Box or crate to stand on or in

⇨ First aid kit (rodents, bugs, and pokey things can happen)

⇨ Prodding tool

⇨ Mace (unlikely that you'll need it, but why not?)

4. Find a friend

Dumpster buddies! There's safety in numbers—there's also fun. The odds are that your special friend is out there waiting, you just have to find him, her, or it. Check out the **"Organizations & Communities"** page on Freegan.info or find your tribe using the plentiful resources at **Trashwiki.org**.

If you come upon a friend when you weren't even looking, just be nice and evaluate their vibe for safety. Some people can get a little possessive over their dumpsters, especially if they're, I dunno, *starving.*

5. Look the part

Yep, there's a part. Think about it: if you look like a friendly, up-standing citizen, employees and security guards are going to be a lot less prone to assuming the worst. They might ignore you or at least ask what you're doing before taking any action. Be kind and honest—tell them about yourself and why you're there. Flash a smile and explain to them that one-third of the world's food is wasted every year and you're just trying to do your part to make things better. Then give them a high five and party on.

6. Timing is everything

Know the hours and the general rhythm of the dumpster's home. Are there scheduled throwaways? There's often a trash splurge right before closing. When is the dumpster emptied? Does Angry Gina take Thursday nights off?

Going after-hours is typically a better way to avoid any uncomfortable run-ins. It's not that getting caught is always a bad thing, though—some stores really do find it helpful or support it from a philanthropic stance. Some even lay out their usable food in anticipation of divers to come!

7. Find the right stuff

If the food needs refrigeration, it's best to avoid it if it's been sitting out for too long (this is where knowing a store's throwaway timing comes in handy). Perishable food is most prone to harmful bacteria when it falls below 40°F (4.4°C). While it's true that expiration dates are mostly a sham, they can still serve as good advice. Use your judgement.

Here are **some safety tips**, but they're just tips. Use them as guidance, not fail-safes.

- ⇨ Strange bulging in the package? The item is fermenting—no dice.
- ⇨ Dented can? There's a chance it's no longer airtight—I'd avoid.
- ⇨ Mold everywhere? Skip it—especially if it's black.
- ⇨ Just a little mold? It's probably okay to skim or cut it off and eat the rest (especially if it's cheese, bread, or fruit).
- ⇨ Sugar-laden food? Sugar's a preservative, go for it (probably).
- ⇨ Avoid fresh meat and meat products.
- ⇨ Packaged breads, grains, baked goods; boxed and canned items; sealed processed foods; and healthy fruits and vegetables are usually safe bets.

8. Leave no trace

Other than, of course, an emptier dumpster. Cleaning up after yourself means that you won't be seen as a nuisance who leaves undesired rubbish in the surrounding area, which also means you'll have better odds of returning without incident.

9. Share!

You're getting free food! Spread the love and spread the word!

10. No trash compactors

This isn't Star Wars Episode IV. Know what I'm sayin!?[8]

Now you know how to safely approach and score the freest of the free food! Ultimately, use your head, don't give dumpster divers a bad name, and remember that there ain't no shame in the game. Wanna up that game? Check out **Trashwiki.org, Freegan.info,** and **"Rob Greenfield's Guide to Dumpster Diving"** at RobGreenfield.tv.

---

[8] https://www.youtube.com/watch?v=7U3Oti2L8S4

⚓ Chapter 19:
⚓ Eat Like You Mean It

Self-prepared meals should be your go-to *when it makes sense*. But ease up on this rule—within reason and mindful of costs—if you're somewhere renowned for its food. As budget-conscious travel-loving foodies, it's a delicate balance when you're trying to save money and sample delicacies all over the world.

I get it. It's fun to walk through a city and simply let your nose guide you. In less-touristy towns, it's usually a safe bet because restaurant owners depend on local repeat customers. In larger cities, though, restaurants often don't care about the experience of foreigners whom they'll never serve again, especially if a prime location guarantees a steady stream of diners.

Still, nothing is more lamentable than wasting money on expensive second-rate meals in first-class destinations! The best restaurant food *isn't* the most expensive. It's a myth and a fallacy if anyone tells you otherwise. But to find the hidden gems, a scan of online peer reviews can net quite a few options regarded as high value for the right price. An hour's worth of online research in Istanbul led me to the best Iskender lamb kebab, minced meat *kofte* lollipops, and pizza-style *lahmacun*. Though these specialties could be found all over the city, advance research led me to the best local spots that didn't overcharge and under-flavor for tourists. Every morsel was money well spent.

You may like to ask a random local for their recommendation—they *must* know, right? They're *local*! But why ask one local when you can ask 20? I have several local friends whose restaurant tastes and preferences I wouldn't trust if I were starving.

These days, with so many resources at our fingertips, your best bet in finding great restaurants is by checking the relevant online communities that permit user ratings and reviews. In the food-rating arena, groups *tend* to come to the correct consensus over an individual, so see if you can find Yelp or the country equivalent to guide you.

All that said, sometimes following the whimsy of one local is the unrivaled path to flavor fulfillment—especially if you use the sharing economy. Yep, numerous locals open their homes (usually for a modest fee) to cook for locals and tourists alike, usually in a group setting. From the grandma home cook, to the amateur dabbler, to the five-star caliber chef, these experiences are one of a kind.

Of course, what would a niche phenomenon like this be without a growing online presence? You can find many of these budding culinarians, their prices, and user reviews on the following **"food tour" websites**:

Mealsharing.com

EatWith.com

WithLocals.com

Feastly.com

Voulezvousdiner.com

Airbnb.com Experiences

Bonappetour.com

If you can't resist the call of the restaurant, there are several **ways to save your money** and create free meals down the road:

⇨ Look for early bird or happy hour specials.

⇨ Check deal sites like LivingSocial or Groupon.

⇨ Search online for "[city name] restaurant discounts/coupons."

⇨ Check international and local restaurant reservation sites for deals (like OpenTable.com).

⇨ Avoid touristy areas, *especially* public squares, plazas, and travel hubs like train or bus stations!

⇨ Make lunch your biggest meal of the day. Prices are typically lower and many countries offer single-priced deals on multi-course meals (*prix fixe* menus) including an appetizer, entree, dessert, and glass of wine or coffee/tea. Usually there's enough food to set some aside for a meal or snack later on.

⇨ Restaurants may try to charge you for sealed bottles if you ask for water, especially if the server knows you're a tourist. Request tap water (if it's safe to drink).

⇨ Unless you *really* trust your concierge, avoid their restaurant recommendations. They probably earn a fee from those restaurants for sending them diners.

Budget Libations

However you grub, invest in a sturdy, lightweight, and (ideally) compact water bottle to avoid buying them on the road—it adds up! Even if you drink the minimum suggested two-liters per day, bottles at $2.50 each equal $75 a month! I suggest a collapsible bottle like a Platypus or Vapur that won't take up space in luggage once it's empty. For less-than-trustworthy local water supplies, invest in a purifying bottle like **LifeStraw Go Water Bottle**.

Speaking of drinks, who of us has gone abroad and *not* sampled a sip of the local spirits? If that's you, *bravo!* Despite how fun it is to say "liquid lunch," in reality, you're probably better off limiting the booze so that you can actually eat food. While that sweet, sweet nectar may help raise a roof or two, it also can liquidate a wallet faster than you can say, *una cerveza por favor*.

If you are going to imbibe, try to stick to happy hour. Some cities offer free food with a glass of beer or wine. To name a few, Granada, San Sebastian, and Milan all let you eat like royalty for the price of one or two measly beers. The amount of food provided is sometimes worth the cost of drinks even if you don't drink the alcohol!

Another strategy if you insist on cocktails is to pre-game. Remember back in the day when we bought booze at a store and got our drank on before going out? It made sense in cash-strapped college, didn't it? It definitely makes sense for budget travel. Make an occasion of it—*responsibly*. Sit on a plaza, beach, or quaint porch and enjoy. Know the open container law. If you're in a country where alcohol is completely illegal, forget you read any of this.

Always keep it safe and enjoy alcohol responsibly!

You've arrived at your departure...

Dearest Travelers,

We've just finished our own journey together, but the big one is just getting started.

It's time to stop standing on the outside looking in. Why be a worker who takes a trip once or twice a year? Instead, remove that touristic looking glass and be a free traveler who *works* once or twice a year.

But remember something for me, k?

Free travel isn't just about your own immediate gratification. That's just an amazing side effect of something much, much bigger. Our special brand of travel, which you may be planning right now, opens up minds, breaks down barriers, smashes prejudice, and yes, makes us better humans.

Free travel brings the world together. It makes this blue green space marble smaller, something you can wrap your arms around. It puts into perspective the trivialities upon which we've placed so much value. That Insta feed just doesn't matter so much when you're sitting atop ancient Grecian ruins while watching the sun set on the Mediterranean Sea.

Just know that imagination, ingenuity, and insight are required. It's the difference between, you know, buying a fish and learning *how* to fish. Between Shark Week on Discovery and cage diving with great whites in South Africa. Between playing Guitar Hero and getting pulled onstage to jam with Jagger.

I hope this book opens doors for you. I hope the experiences of us free travelers will allow you to start seeing the world however you wish. Because now, with this book, you have no excuses.

Okay—*fine*—maybe that big project is due soon or you're about to have a baby or it's the Super Bowl, but *after* that ...

Get out there, Sporto!

Happy Trails!

Acknowledgments

Years and years to produce this tiny thing, and the ways and names of those who've helped seem like they could fill the pages of this very book.

My parents: if you didn't love travel, I probably wouldn't love travel. If you didn't love me, I'd have a much harder time loving me. You were the start and remain the follow-through, and you supported this book from day one!

John Amory, aka Mr. Jams, for helping me kickstart all of this, for confidence-boosting, putting up with me, and general partner-in-criming.

Another John: Mr. Dinatale, for many of the same same reasons, but different. You are a word master and a million times more selfless than you pretend, and through you I found Mrs. Amanda Brennan, a creative master who designed the ultimate cover and gave me a million invaluable ideas because it's the only language she speaks.

My Goose, who never questioned the hours and hours of time and angst spent earning no money while creating this baby.

Richard Downie and James Toth, my boiz at Fanciful Fox—ever-grateful that you consistently put up with me and helped me make the best promo video ever. Adam Skolnick and John Moore: You gave my brain space to think of something bigger—the open ocean brought to my mind.

Jason Moore and Rob Greenfield, you both took a chance on me and had no idea who I was, and I'm endlessly lucky that y'all came aboard. The world needs more of you!

Douglas Preston, who lent his industry-knowledge and a very busy hand to help perfect my pitch. Aša Ricciardi: My first editor, a fellow nomad, speaker of shared language. May there be many more to come! Sam Title: My editing magician for voice and chutzpah—all the LOLs are for you. Joy Xiang & Margarita Martinez: Fellow explorers, word-lovers, and proofreaders extraordinaire. Ljiljana Pavkov: you brought me through the finish line by designing this book with generosity and unparalleled creative agility! Rakesh Ranjan: a web designer of brilliant talent and personality—I hope to meet you again on the interwebs!

The first Beta readers who suffered through a horrendous first draft: Brian Foster, Phillipa Telford, Arthur Fogartie, and Clare Luebbert. The next Betas who who suffered through a still-horrendous fourth draft: Cat Commander, Mark Royer, Michael Galvis-Ralston, Maria Hilliger, Andrew Tierce, Kristina Nikolic, Chel Barnes.

Chel Barnes again, for being a fellow traveler and inspirational badass. Charles and Ellie, for your humor, kindness, and hosting. Jake Berton, for your technical support and generosity along the way. Derek Sivers, for introducing me to distilled writing and inspiring a crucial rework. Manfred Yon, for inadvertently giving me the title for this book!

Other friends and lovelies who shared valuable opinions for nothin': Colin Smith, Aragorn Fenton, Kristin Rider, Willie Handler.

The many who helped fund this book: John Gilkey (and how the Idiot Workshop and Wet the Hippo influenced my words), Elaine & Art Kaiser, Benjamin Ralston, Sumir Karayi, Sandy Flint, Dick Duncan Downie, Randy & Amy Buckspan, Jeffrey Grellman, Patrick Nolan, Aragorn Fenton, Jonathan Sparks, Patrick McGee, Noah Tabakin, Adam Petke, Meggan Kimberley, Beverly Woodruff, Jonny Cruz, John-Michael Triana, Anne Ulseth, Matt Tosi, Morgan Meadows, Jason Heutmaker, Amy King, Jason Evans, Clare Venner, Jason Poston, Brett Shirley, Lauren Malkani, Martelle & Prudence Daniels, Chris & Elizabeth Kaiser, Ronnie Adrian, Dorian Frankel, Carole Foran, Christine Owens, Max Baumgarten . . . but that's not all! Check out the Wall of Thanks at EverywhereForNothing.com to see the rest!

Finally, to all the fellow travelers and hosts I've met along the way. Your spirit is here in these pages and you are not forgotten. Keep fighting the good fight!

Author Bio

Meggan is a writer, writing coach, foodie, and modern nomad in Atlanta, Georgia. From north Georgia (Calhoun, hello!), she's lived in Jackson Hole, Los Angeles, Santa Fe, Portland, and various places abroad for bits of time. Find her and connect at Bossmeggan.com or EverywhereForNothing.com. She'd love to hear from you!

Want More Free Travel?

As a thank-you for reading this book, I'm offering you something exclusive: (1) The option to connect with me directly about your personal travel questions, and (2) insider info handpicked and delivered to your inbox.

Let's do this – visit everywherefornothing.com/readers

Index and References

Please visit EverywhereForNothing.com for updated versions of this book's index and references.

Made in the USA
Lexington, KY
23 October 2019